SELL AND GROW RICH

SELL AND GROW RICH

SALES MANTRAS FOR A SUCCESSFUL LIFE AND BUSINESS

Bhupenddra Singh Raathore

An imprint of
Srishti Publishers & Distributors

Srishti Publishers & Distributors
A unit of AJR Publishing LLP
212A, Peacock Lane
Shahpur Jat, New Delhi – 110 049

editorial@srishtipublishers.com

First Published by Bold,
an imprint of Srishti Publishers & Distributors in 2023

10 9 8 7 6 5 4 3 2 1

This is a work of non-fiction, based on the authors' experiences and life-learning. The results of the recommendations given herein may vary from case to case. The views and opinions expressed in the work are the author's own and the facts are as reported by him, and the publisher is in no way liable for the same.

Printed and bound in India

Dedicated to

My Family, Friends, Mentors, Gurus,
Team, Community and Everyone
who has ever been in Sales.

And everyone who will ever
be in the most lucrative skill of all time - Sales.

Contents

Preface ix

Introduction xi

Chapter 1:
Why Sales? 1

Chapter 2:
What is Sales? 17

Chapter 3:
So, are you ready to be a Sales Professional? 27

Chapter 4:
Getting Ready – Habits of a good Sales Professional 35

Chapter 5:
Sales as a Science – Sales Processes for assured results! 47

Chapter 6:
Sales as an Art – Soft skills you should master 73

Chapter 7:
Importance of asking the right questions in Sales 93

Chapter 8:
Human Needs and Sales 115

Chapter 9:
Sales models and Techniques 129

Contents

Preface

Being a breakthrough strategist, trainer, coach and author for people and enterprises, I am in touch with various people on regular basis.

I have seen one common pattern among people – they all 'wish' to be successful.

Most of the people want to make it big in life. Theyhave an idealistic image of doing something great in life. They want to do something on their own and have the goal of helping people transform their life. Many talk of making this country bigger and giving employment to others. In my 'Discover Your Vision' programme, I meet many people who have a lofty vision to make the world better.

They have an idealistic view of the future of the world they want to create.

But subsequently, I see just a few meeting their goals and making it big in life, business and career.

Ever wondered what is the reason behind the failure of a majority of these visionaries?

It's one word – Selling Skills.

You can build a powerful product or content and feel excited about it, but if you can't 'transfer this flame of excitement' in the heart and mind of others, it's all meaningless.

I have seen so many people finally retreating and going back to their old and average life, just because they could not sell.

Just because they could not understand the secrets of selling their idea, product or service to others.

Just because they misunderstood their target group.

Just because they could not understand the pricing correctly.

Or because they kept on thinking of building a large mass of followers around them.

Because they could not design their 'sales funnel'.

Because they could not come out of their 'zone of shyness' to sell and grow their community base.

Thereasons could be many, but in short – Theycould not succeed in life, just because they could not become a good sales person.

It pains me because I know they actually had a great idea, product or service which had the potential to transform the world. And it could not happen just because of one shortcoming – their inability to sell.

Even Thomas Alva Edison would have been lost into oblivion had he not been a great businessman who knew how to market and sell his inventions. Being a scientist would not have helped him much.

That is how powerful and impactful the art and science of selling is.

Thefact is – everyone can sell. And I kept wondering how I could make it easy for people to sell and grow rich. That's when I decided to write a book which could become a 'pocketbook of learning and excelling' in sales.

I will stop here.

Let your reading the experience say it aloud.

That you can *Sell and Grow Rich*.

Introduction

There are several books on Sales in the market already! So why one more?

A few readers might be thinking on these lines, I am sure. Especially those who do not know me well, or have connected with me just recently.

But anyone who knows me well or has been connected with me through one of those numerous programmes which I have been conducting over the last many years, would know that *if there was one book which must have come from me, it had to be a book on Sales!*

Wonder why?

Because, all that I have attained in life by the grace of god, blessings of my mentors and people who are connected with me – recognition, name, fame, money, etc – is primarily due to my teachings on Sales. I have been conducting many programmes on communication skills, discovering one's vision, commando training, public speaking, leadership, outbound team bonding, among others, but if there is one topic around which I have done the maximum programmes – it is Sales.

This book *had* to come because it is based on tried and tested principles on Sales – all of which I have personally implemented in my life and career. It does not contain mere theory. I have not written a single principle which I have personally not implemented and which has not given me the desired results. I have not kept any secrets and have revealed it all in this book. These practical tips have worked for me and I am sure these are going to work for everyone who reads, reflects and begins taking actions based on what I have shared in this book.

Those who have been connected with me for more than a decade might have been waiting for this book. But even those who have come to be connected with me more recently, know that once they finish this book, they will experience that this is the most powerful and outcome-based book coming from me.

The book has both the art and science behind Sales.

The book has many workable tools which you can use to enhance your prowess as a sales professional.

We have segregated the book in simple to understand chapters.

The goal is just one – to help many people convert their dreams into reality and be successful in life, business and career.

I would be happy to hear your feedbacks on the book.

The Beginning of Everything

People say that the world's best success stories emerge out of almost nothing! The pain of nothingness creates a hunger. People also call it burning desire, which is so badly needed for extraordinary stories.

Mine is a story in the making, but all that I have given to the universe so far is because of that pain which I still remember.

Picture a little boy born in a traditional lower middle-class family in a small village on the edge of an arid desert land. That was me, who knew the pain of nothingness and hollowness. The village was Khatoli in Kishangarh district of Rajasthan. I completed my education from the government school in Kishangarh. After completing my schooling,

I was keen on supporting my father as he was the sole bread earning member in the family. Constantly thinking of how I could support my father, I tried my hands in many interviews. Destiny seemed to be working overtime to make me realize the pain deeply. You ask why? Guess what? I got rejected in every interview that I appeared for. My academic credentials were not bad, but I belonged to that unending crowd of people who come from average or average plus financial background and look, speak and struggle like every other person.

I was not able to secure even a mediocre job. Like every young man of my age, I wanted to get everything my family dreamt of a big and beautiful house, a new car, properties and a comfortable bank balance. However, it all seemed a distant dream, given my reality back then. I was dreaming of being a millionaire, but in reality, I was not even able to secure a menial job!

Do you find this relatable? Hold on, there is a lot you are going to connect with.

Life seemed hopeless and I used to believe that I would never make it to the millionaire league in my life. Theonly prevalent thoughts were those of hopelessness and suicide.

Yes, you read it right. The thought of ending it all had started drifting in my head.

The suicidal thoughts reached a level where I also tried to find out the easiest, quickest and most effortless options to end my life. Finally, I zeroed in on committing suicide on the railway tracks passing through those dusty deserts. Just lie down and close your eyes. That's it!

Now you see the connection – I was in pain because I wanted it all easy and quick, even death.

I thought that I will be free from all the burden with zero survival chances and everything will be sorted once and for all.

I left home for the railway tracks with a clouded and upset mental state. But somehow, I could not attempt a suicide that day and thought of doing it the next day.

Now you see another connection – in those days, I postponed things one after the other, including... You know it by now 😊.

While returning home, I was all lost in my thoughts when I heard someone behind me shout, "*Bahut bada aadmi banega tu*". At first, I did not pay attention to it as no one there seemed to know me. A few seconds later, I heard the same words, "*Bahut bada aadmi banega tu*". I turned towards the voice and saw a well-built person, almost 6 feet in height, wearing a kurta pyjama looking at me and saying those words. I still wasn't sure if he was talking to me. For the third time, he repeated, "*Tujhse hi bol raha hoon, bahut bada aadmi banega tu*".

These words gave me a jolt to bring me back to the moment and made me conscious about my surrounding.

He was a part of the procession carried out by the transgender community. I got scared, as coming across a complete stranger after what I was going to do seemed a bit off and unnerving to me. There were many people walking on that street, but he pointed out only me and said those words.

Now my thoughts had changed. From the pictures of railway tracks, I was thinking about the words said by the person.

When I reached home and sat at the dinner table, a look at my siblings and my parents was enough to help me realize the blunder I was going to commit today. The mere thought of what my family would have gone through, had I acted on my suicidal thoughts, filled me with remorse and guilt to an unending extent. I couldn't sleep that night. The entire episode of the happenings of the day kept repeating itself in my thoughts, and I was trying hard to decipher it, but couldn't figure out much. Those words kept repeating in my mind like a broken record.

Those words had transformed something within me that night. Today as I write this, I can say that it was the most welcome change, to say the least.

That turned out to be the decisive turning of my life and I said to myself that from today onwards, "जो भी करूंगा कमाल का करूंगा।"

From that day onwards, I made sure that every action of mine was aimed at the well-being of my family. Going forward, "Doing was the only option; dying was not an option at all".

Filled with new awakenings, I enrolled myself for a 3-year course in Computers from NIIT. I topped the batch for three years in a row.

Filled with renewed confidence, I went for an interview, but again got rejected. The chain of rejections kept growing longer with every interview I appeared in. The reason that I could figure out was my low confidence, and this series of rejections filled me with utter disappointment and depression. In one of the interviews I was insulted badly for lack of fluent English-speaking skills. That insult hit my self-respect and I decided to conquer the language within three months.

Certainly, despite rejections, I was a different man now. I was taking rejections as challenges instead of giving it up.

I started training for spoken English skills under the guidance of two exemplary English trainers, and with their unconditional support and my relentless effort, I mastered the language within three months. This gave me a new lease of confidence and a successful shot at the interview. I got selected in one of the top BPOs in the country. This exposure in the BPO helped me polish my communication skills further, as I was communicating with Americans, Brits and Australians.

I was satisfied with my life and earning enough to fulfil my basic needs with ease when someone told me about the skill of Public Speaking and the exponential growth opportunities that would come along.

One day, someone told me about a course on Public Speaking. I had now become a man of action and enrolment for that course kick-started the next phase of my life, which I am living right now.

After the workshop, I was certain that this was something I wanted to do for the rest of my life, but the fear of quitting a well-paying job to start afresh was also there. I was already in a confident space and I knew that I could make it as an exceptional Public Speaker. Within a few days of starting public speaking, I started getting very good opportunities and even better compliments. My teacher taught me never to back off from going on stage, whether it is for mimicry, dancing, singing, or any other activity. Though I was not a good dancer or a singer, but I still used to try everything and this helped me boost my confidence.

Soon the day came when I decided to go with my decision of starting a career as a Trainer and Public Speaker. This was not at all an easy journey, though it has fared well for me.

As a Corporate Trainer, I was doing pretty well, but I was not able to scale up my domain. I was still far from my dream car and house. In one of my upcoming workshops, I was about to witness another dramatic turn of events in my life.

It was the year 2012. I was delivering a session and one person soon got up to leave the session.

I asked him the reason to leave and he said something that gave me yet another jolt.

"You are talking about success, and I don't see your success. So why should I listen to you ... ?"

Only 15-20 participants were there in that workshop. I had worked very hard to organize that session and this incident took place right in the beginning of the session.

I couldn't understand what to say to this person. So, I asked him, "What do you mean by success?"

He asked in return, "Which car do you drive?"

I said, "Maruti Suzuki Ritz."

He said, "I drive a Honda City. Do you have your own house in Pune?"

I said, "No. I stay on rent at Bhavani Peth and pay rupees four thousand monthly."

He laughed and just left. I could somehow manage the situation.

I was filled with anger as I never thought people could be so cold and mean.

But when I thought rationally that evening, I realized that the person was correct.

This incident left an indelible mark on me. I realized that I will have to achieve big to make people believe in what I was sharing with them. People want to see the evidence of success, or else they would never trust my words. My journey of making people successful was a bumpy ride till I became a huge success myself. I started to work for more hours and conducted more sessions, but despite working relentlessly, I wasn't able to scale up.

A few days of self-analysis helped me find the root cause behind this problem.

I wasn't selling high ticket products. Only high-ticket products could help me scale my revenue and profits faster. I was already delivering the best content, and the participants were very happy with the services and quality. All I had to do was design a high-ticket product.

I designed a 6-figure product and went to meet my existing clients as I was damn sure that I will close a minimum of twenty people in a month. A month later, I was standing at zero closings. The high-ticket game is an entirely different game and you don't just require a super hero product (actually an assured solution to customers' problem) for this segment, but also a whole different set of skills to understand the buyer's psychology and excellent selling skills.

I had the first two characteristics, but I lacked the selling ability, because I had recruited a sales crew to do the work. I was never into successful sales; it was handled by the sales team. I've realized that I can't rely on people to help me progress.

I learnt the skill of sales and mastered it through consistent practice. It definitely took time to master this skill, but it was worth every hour I spent on this. Every challenge and every rejection in sales played a key part in my success as one of the best Sales professionals and trainers in the country.

I might have never realized the importance of this skill, had I not witnessed that incident. I am forever thankful to that guy.

This is the story of my journey from nothingness to all that the world in general associates with success. Luxury cars, villas, bank balance, love from people and a community of millions who get inspired from my work.

It was all possible due to my selling skills, and this book is all about that one skill which will make you the king of your life.

Chapter 1
Why Sales?

You are holding this book because of one reason, you want to master the skill of sales. You somehow know that Sales is the only profession in the world which can fulfil all the dreams of your life.

However, many people give up. Many people quit because sales is really difficult. It requires time, effort, and suffering. It requires consistent practice. Let me give you the reasons you must master this skill:

1. This skill can give you a lot of money.
2. This skill can give you the freedom you are looking for.
3. Sales people are required in every single organization in the world.
4. There is no other profession which can give you so much knowledge in a short span of time.
5. There is no other profession that can make you as rough and tough as this one.
6. The profession of sales really makes you people-friendly.
7. It gives you the ability to understand the psychology of people.

8. It makes you a better and more powerful human being.
9. It will be helpful in every single domain of life and business.

Now you might be wondering whether Bhupenddra Singh Raathore himself has got the benefits which he has just written above.

The answer is an emphatic, loud and clear YES!

Yes. I was earning only Rs 1,200 per month and today this profession helps me earn Rs 2.5 crore, monthly! I have been able to generate one crore rupees in an hour, which happened in a Sales webinar which I conducted on 9th May 2021. When the world was worried about restrictions related to the pandemic, it was this profession which kept me flying higher and higher. Never for a day did I look back and feel like a victim, unlike millions of others.

This is the power of Sales as a profession. For those who believe in re-incarnation, I would like to be a sales professional again and again.

I think, you have got a sense of how powerful Sales is! It is this profession which gives me the power and ability to think of creating wellness retreats worth Rs 15 crore and buy houses and cars which I could never even have dreamt of without this profession.

You might be wondering, but can others also make the kind of money I have made?

One of the participants of my Sales programmes, Shailendra Devangan, who works in Real Estate, sold properties worth Rs 30 crore in three days and earned a commission of Rs 35 lakh.

There is another participant, Santosh Pal, who is earning more than Rs 2 crore profit every year. Earlier he was earning close to

Rs 50,000. I will be covering these two stories in detail towards the end of this chapter.

You can see videos on my YouTube channel (@coachBSR) for many success stories. This will emphasize on the point that Sales can turn around the life of anyone who truly follows what I am going to talk about in this book.

Let me tell you a few stories in brief.

Let us begin with the story of a trainer Salman Khan. He had seen the days when he went bankrupt. His house and other properties were on the verge of being sold off.

Then, he joined my Sales programme and followed all the suggested actions.

He had a business of INR 30 lakhs in 2021, which included both online and offline modes. He first contacted me in the year 2022. In the year 2022, he rebuilt his INR 1 crore business. You can watch my interview with him where he says – "In the year 2020, I had to return money to the lenders. The pandemic came, and all the businesses started closing. I was totally clueless. I joined your 'Magic of Thinking Rich' workshop – India's biggest 28-day free live online workshop. I started working on the mindset. I stopped watching all news channels. I now knew, I had to go online. I decided to start with old clients who used to visit us in our old programmes in hotels and conference halls. I decided to use my mobile phone and started conducting programmes through Facebook. In the very first month, I closed a sale with a hundred people and earned a little more than Rs 2 lakh which helped me pay my debts. I knew, I needed to have a coach. I wanted to pay Rs 12 lakhs, but did not have the money. I started hearing inspiring podcasts and saying affirmations. I finally decided to sell my wife's jewellery and join the course. I thank my wife for all the support."

The amazing thing about Salman Khan is that despite having attended my programmes on Sales, he still joins my 'Discover Your Vision', 'Public Speaking', and other programmes. Despite being a good trainer himself, he is still joining my programmes to learn more and be better. He also brings his wife and child to all of the retreats. His wife is now in charge of his marketing efforts. His family is also expressing his opinions, and the whole family is making progress. His wife and child are discovering at a young age what Salman and many others discovered much later in life.

Let me tell you the story of my first tryst with the field of Sales. My first Sales Guru was a little girl who was selling books on the streets of Pune.

Yes, you heard it right!

"Hi sir, how are you?" Her voice was exuberant.

"I am wonderful ma'am but sorry, I don't think I have met you earlier." I said trying my best not to hurt her and bring her energy down.

"No sir, we are meeting for the first time," she added further. "I will just take three minutes and twenty-one seconds of yours and will tell you what will change your life and business forever."

"Yes, please go ahead . . . ," I said, still a bit hesitatingly.

"Sir, I know you have many big dreams and you want to fulfil all your dreams. You want to be a great success in life. You love your family a lot and want to make them proud . . ."

Then, she asked me many questions whose answers were always in affirmation. For example:

"Sir, you are a very intelligent person. Right or wrong?"

"Sir, you love your parents a lot. Right or wrong?"

You know, no one will give a 'no' as an answer.

I did not know then, but now I know she was asking me 'agreement frame questions' about which you will know later in this book.

"Sir, the rich house is not the one where there is lot of money. It is the one where there is a huge library. Do you agree?"

"Yes," I said smilingly.

"Sir, I want you to have a full set of enriching books..." She said before waiting to see my curiosity and making a huge offer of discount.

One thing led to another and I ended up buying the books.

It was 7 in the evening and darkness had set in. This appeared to be her last sale of the day.

"Its 7 p.m. now. What time did you start your day and how many books have you sold so far?" I was growing curious. I must admit – I was inspired with her energy and confidence.

"Sir, I leave home at 7:30 in the morning and reach office by 8:30. There is an energy building session and then we have our breakfast in the office. After that, we leave the office to sell our books. I make the first call/presentation at 10 a.m." She said with her face beaming with excitement. I failed to notice any tiredness on her face.

"You have been selling the books over last nine hours! How many books have you been able to sell?" I asked.

"Sir, I have given 112 presentations so far..." She smiled.

"How many books have you sold so far?" I was embarrassed at being so direct, but somehow could not suppress the urge.

"Sir, only five so far...," she said.

"Only five? This means 107 rejections so far. Is it true?" I was finding it unbelievable.

"Yes sir," her smile had turned deeper.

"So how do you still smile after receiving 107 rejections? How do you maintain this high level of energy?" I was not going to leave it unless I discovered the secret of her confidence and persistence.

"Sir, we have been taught that we are the first for every new customer. Hence, every time I talk to a new customer, I can't carry the disappointment of the last failed attempt at selling while talking to a new customer. We have been taught this strongly and repeatedly. First impression is the last impression ..."

Wow. That is great; first impression is the last impression.

"But how do you maintain such a high energy, despite hearing so many negatives?"

"Sir, it's simple. I do not hear a *no* at all. For me, a no means Next Opportunity. And I simply move on to the next customer. No heartburns. No regret. No frustrations." She had said something incredible.

I was dumbstruck with her selling skills.

"Don't you sometimes get frustrated? Don't you think of leaving sales?" I asked.

"That's an easy question. Yes, every day in the evening, I feel like leaving this profession. But every day in the morning, we do affirmations, meditation, visualization and reading of goal along with energy building. Then again, I am recharged to be in this field, which keeps it exciting for me.

"Great! I loved your presentation. How do you make such a strong presentation?" I asked her.

"Sir, I am not here to sell, but to add value. I am always confident in the value my product or service will provide to individuals. I am confident in my product, which makes me unstoppable. It keeps me going. In the initial stage, it is difficult and I actually used to cry after hearing words of anger and rejection from my customer. Then I learnt that for every salesperson, understanding and handling rejections in the key.

Then I asked, "Why don't you leave all that you are doing? Would you like to join me as a sales person?"

"No sir, you can't afford me." I was stunned to hear her as she spoke about a luxury car she drove, a great home where she lived and the foreign trip which she had planned for her family.

Years have passed by, but that experience is still my guiding light.

That day, I knew if she could make it, anyone in this world can!

And I was right.

Now, would you like to be the master in the field of Sales?

Then start with a powerful visualization to keep you going as you walk on this path of greatness.

Let me tell you Shailendra's story in greater detail. Shailendra Devangan's success story is nearly amazing; he sold plots and properties for Rs 30 crores in just three days. Of course, these three days have come after a journey of learning and taking action for more than a decade. He has been connected with me as a regular participant in various programmes over the last many years. He comes from a humble background, where he has seen days of sharing one bicycle with his family members. Of course, it's a different time now, when he owns a fleet of six cars, all earned through hard work and continuous learning and improvement. Shailendra joined my course, and he found it transformational. He joined other courses, including 'Discover Your Vision' and 'Business Tycoon Manufacturing Process' and started making fast changes in his life. He made some breakthrough changes in his thought process and living patterns. He became a guy who accepted responsibility, stopped blaming the world for his mistakes, began spending time with inspiring people, altered his behaviours, and began practising sales on a daily basis.

He is the owner of a company 'Shaurya Infratech' in Raipur. By his own admission, thinking big was the first habit he learnt. He had also joined my 'Commando Training' programme and was a regular attendee at my morning sessions. He actually exceeded my expectations. I used to ask people to join my sessions at 5 a.m., Shailendra started waking up an hour earlier at 4 a.m. Not only that, he had Facebook Live sessions between 4 and 5 a.m. Gradually, he inspired people. He took quick action and launched his YouTube channel. He started recording and uploading many videos to his YouTube channel. He began providing people value by allowing them to buy good houses for free. As people began to reap the benefits, they began to recommend his name to others, and people began to seek him out. Shailendra continued to attend my 'Discover Your Vision' session once a year. He shown a strong desire to improve his ideas and skill sets. He makes me proud to be his mentor today. To summarize, going by his own admission, Shailendra has made three transformations in his life as follows:

- Think big. Do not think small. Always compare yourself with the best of people. Be in the company of people better than you. He attended many property seminars in bigger cities to uplift his thinking process.

- Build powerful habits. From waking up early in the morning to learning every day, Shailendra believed in making regular positive changes as a person.

- Learn skills. Shailendra learnt Public Speaking, Sales, Relationship building and other skills to attain success that he has gained.

Let's look at another magical story of Santosh Pal.

Santosh Pal has been waking up at 4 a.m. every day ever since he has been there with me after joining my programme. He started practicing the lessons which I taught and also joined other programmes. In fact, he became a regular joiner in my 'Discover Your Vision' programme. Every year, he began attending my similar programmes. That demonstrated his eagerness to learn. His monthly salary at work was Rs 50,000. He mustered the bravery to quit his work, but he never left my firm. He is now at a point in his life where he is earning a net profit of more than 10-12 lakh rupees per month from his chosen business of real estate.

"If you want to do big things, you have to take big decisions," he quotes this sentence which he had noted in one of the programmes. Today he has gained courage to hold 'Aawas Mela' (House fair) and sold forty properties in one day, thereby getting revenue of multiple crores in one day. He started with selling 3-4 properties in a month, and today, he is selling forty properties in a day. He had a revenue of ten crore rupees in just one day and that resulted in a profit of rupees 12 lakhs in one day!

Imagine the transformation – from Rs 50,000 in a month to Rs 10 lakhs in a day! Unbelievable? But with the profession of Sales, it's absolutely believable!

Let me share another story of a mentee. I interviewed him recently.

> *I was doing things randomly till I met you and understood how powerful having a vision in life could be. I had left my job and was doing something on my own for the last three years. I was struggling to rise beyond a point. I was surrounded by people who were either doing job or were struggling like me. I knew, I needed a guru or coach. When I met you, I found a spark in you. I realized that you speak from the heart and I knew I needed to be coached by you. I went for your 2-days programme 'Discover Your Vision' and then I realized that my core was away from what I was doing. I was training people. My core was to add value to organizations at a global level by helping them expand their exports. I immediately shut my old business of training as it was hardly giving me a profit of Rs 50-60,000 per month. I focused on exports and import and became an EXIM coach. Since this field was close to my heart, I kept learning more and build on my already obtained body of knowledge over the last many years.*
>
> *Then I recalled your talk where you had said, 'You should automate your business so that you earn even when you are asleep.'*
>
> *That was when I got the idea of developing a web-based platform on which by filling one form, 25-26 different documents could get ready at the same time. I had learnt by then that for exporting one product, twenty-five odd agencies were getting involved, it'd be great! It was a cumbersome process and if I could solve this*

problem. This platform was recognized at the national level in the presence of Prime Minister Modi Ji and Mr Piyush Goyal. I will never forget that day of 15th January 2022.

To avoid sitting on my previous work, I went ahead and constructed another platform for automating the preparation of any document linked to the formation of a corporation or the export or import of any goods. Visit the website, click on the link relevant to the need, submit the appropriate documents, and make the payment. Then our team goes to work. Nobody needs to call or message me because the process is completely automated. In the process, I became a speaker with the Government of India. I have been conducting stage talks in various cities like Dubai, Aurangabad, Jalna and many other cities. Being an official speaker on behalf of the Government of India's Exports department is a matter of extreme pride for me. These tours are fully sponsored by the Government of India.

Anyone who has seen my interview with Vinayak Temgire on my YouTube channel 'Coach BSR', has felt extremely inspired.

There are many stories and let me tell you one more in the series. This is the story of Deepak and Nisha Jain who are siblings and the founder of Anokha Brain Pvt Ltd.

The duo came from a humble family background. They did not even have proper food to eat. Their father owned a hand cart.

They joined my programme 'Discover Your Vision' in Lonavala where they created a goal of earning one crore rupees per year. Today, they have a team of fifteen people and have closed the last year with a revenue of three crore rupees. This means, they have crossed their vision of the original one crore rupees by 200%. Their next goal is to reach a revenue of one million dollars, i.e. eight crore rupees by 31st December 2023. They have planned a grand event for 10,000 people on 12th August 2025.

Their journey consists of three remarkable points:

Vision

Goals

Disruption

It is because of these three qualities that Deepak and Nisha Jain who started their journey with a programme of Rs 750, now have programmes worth Rs 3 lakh. They are running fifteen different programmes now and are super excited about what they have achieved. They started two years ago when they did not even know how to conduct a webinar and today, they have touched a revenue of a whopping 3 crore rupees.

Let me now tell you the story of Amit Kamboj. He has turned his business from a loss of INR 20 lakh to a profit of INR 1 crore.

In his own words, he had burnt the bridges. He did not want to go back to a job, rather decided to keep moving ahead while being an entrepreneur and export/import trainer. He recalls the day he was in a negative 20 lakh predicament. In the year 2020, he enrolled in my commando training; that proved to be a watershed moment in his life. He started beginning his day with positive morning affirmations. He wrote goals that I proposed. He began to shift his mentality from negative to positive. He started his online training programme on 15th June 2020 when only four people joined his course. Now coming to the magical part – till the mid of 2022, i.e. within two years, he had trained 1000 companies and individuals through paid programmes. He also conducts free sessions and thereby, he has trained 35,000 people so far.

He has 270 ratings for his shows, all of which are five stars. He was in a difficult situation after a loss of INR 20 lakhs. He did not have any other option but to design his own social media campaigns. He created his own Sales Funnel, Facebook ad and online systems.

Today, he gives the full credit to the following two 'M' factors:

- Have a focused and positive Mindset.
- Begin your day on a positive note. Master your morning time to Master your day.

Today, he aspires to contribute to India's goal of reaching a five-trillion-dollar economy. He strongly believes that this target can only be achieved through promoting exports. He also has a vision of helping one lakh people set up their exports business.

This is the power of this book that gives me an unstoppable purpose to keep writing such a book which has the true potential to transform lives.

Not just professional success, you also become a superior person. Sales makes you a better human being.

- Sales makes you a stronger person by teaching you how to deal with rejection. Despite the criticism, you maintain a positive attitude. Sales allows you to develop greater connections because you interact with people on a daily basis, both in wins and losses.

- Sales gives you a lot of confidence because you win individuals and orders based on your own strengths.
- You write your own cheques in sales.
- Sales allows you to earn enough money to do things that broaden your perspective. I go to many regions of the world to see and learn from other people and places.

The Hero in Sales

Every movie has a hero. Can you think of a movie without a hero? I am sure you can't. When you are selling a product, you need to treat your customer like a hero. Marketers are practicing this in all areas and with all products. Examples could be:

You drink Mountain Dew and you will be the hero in life.

You drink Boost and you will be a hero like Sachin Tendulkar.

You drive the car of a certain make just like a hero drives.

You buy a villa from a premium builder and live the life of a hero.

You buy the course of leadership development and become a hero in your professional environment.

Keep this concept in mind and treat your customers like heroes. You will make more sales than you earlier used to do.

A Powerful Visualization

Imagine that you are living the life of your dreams. This is the life you always wanted to have. You are living in a villa or a condominium you always wanted to live in. It has the required number of rooms and amenities. It has the kind of luxury you once dreamt of, including wall hangings, swimming pool, huge terraces and gardens which give you a feeling of fulfilment. Your family is proud of your achievements. Your kids are studying in international schools and are living in some of the best cities one can think of.

You are going on vacations to multiple locations around the world. You are able to invest money and your money makes even more money every month. You see your wealth growing. You live a life which is fulfilling and have enough with you to contribute to make others' life awesome and great.

Your interviews are published on the front page of national journals and you are a regular face on television and news channels. You get congratulatory messages from your old friends and family members every now and then. It feels so great to know that there are so many willing to be like you and live your kind of life. You have a private movie theatre in your house in which you enjoy your childhood videos and movies along with your family. You provide employment to a large number of people in the society and you feel great to be their life support system.

You have been awarded on the stage in reputed forums. You fly to some of the best cities in business class and make new friends every now and then. People want to be around you and you get respected wherever you go. People invite you to give keynote speeches on how to excel in the field of Sales. When you speak about your journey of success in sales, others listen with rapt attention. You get applauded in the auditorium every now and then during your talks.

You have the freedom of time, money, and mobility. You have more than enough money; you have time to spend doing things you enjoy, and you can travel anywhere in the world at your leisure. How do you feel?

Visualization is essential. Every now and then, remind yourself of your ideal day. It will undoubtedly propel you to the pinnacle of salespersonship. I wish you the best of success as you begin your journey of implementing some of the key lessons that you are going to read in this book.

Please read the full book. Don't stop in between as this book will be your best friend for sure and you will thank yourself forever for this decision of yours. If needed, read the book twice, take notes and keep these written in your office so that you are reminded of practicing these again and again, till you are a great success.

After all, that was the ultimate goal behind writing this book.

Chapter 2
What is Sales?

Let's understand what Sales truly is?

Before I go any further, let me ask you a question: if you know that someone from an insurance company, network marketing company, real estate, or any other profession is approaching you and wanting an appointment, what do you think of that person? I have asked this question in many of my live workshops and I get the following answers:

He will cheat me!

He is going to be boring and will try to loot me with his product!

He will waste my time!

I will have to hear his boring sales presentation!

He will try to trap me with his sweet talks...

And some more thoughts like the above ones.

Do you also get the similar thoughts?

Ha ha ha... 😊

This is the reality.

Now one of the reasons why many people don't like to sell is because these thoughts keep running in their mind the moment they think about sales as a profession.

Hence, even if the sales is one of the most rewarding professions, people tend to keep away from this.

Here is the time to break these negative thought patterns and look at the entire sales from a fresh perspective.

I have had more than a decade of intense working experience in Sales and here are my 'Ten Commandments of Sales'. As you go through these, you will also see me shatter some myths related to sales.

Here we go:

1. Selling is Helping

You might be having some negative thoughts while thinking of the word sales. These thoughts could be:

Sales is deceiving others into buying or it means pestering others and making their life hell.

Or sales means being hated and rejected by people.

Sales means pain and suffering on daily basis.

So here is the truth! None of the above is true. Someone who sold me a course on selling worth Rs 7,500 in 2007 has helped me earn more than Rs 75 crore in a decade. And before that, I earned Rs 25 lakh in ten years... isn't it magical!

Did he cheat me or did he help me? He actually helped me beyond my imagination. Not only did I earn 75 crores in the last decade, I also got a chance to impact the lives of more than a crore people. I got an opportunity to address the whole world from the United Nations headquarter in New York City. I was awarded at many forums and got a chance to write many books.

Many people carry this misconception in their mind and heart that the profession of selling is bad. They hate selling. Even I used to despise selling and would rather sit alone and watch my business fail than try to sell. I also had this negative mindset against selling, till I attended some programmes, meditated over the idea of selling and got clarity. Then I realized that selling is the core of progress in this world. Now I can say with confidence to the whole world that - selling is helping.

When a person sells a wrist watch, he makes someone's life run on time. He makes the life of customer more organized and time bound. Isn't it?

When a newspaper vendor sells his product to someone, he makes the person better informed. Am I right?

When a person sells a book to someone, he makes someone a better person with more knowledge.

A person who sells light bulb brings light to your home.

A person selling AC makes your life cool.

A person who sells a course on selling, makes someone a better salesperson.

These are just a few examples.

And who is not selling in this world?

Even spiritual gurus are selling their products/courses.

Someone is selling meditation. Someone is selling *pranik* healing to make someone happier and healthier. Someone is selling yoga courses to help people get healthier. Someone is selling herbal products to make you better.

So, put this belief in your mind that when you are selling the right product, which is useful for your family and others, then you are helping the person. So, selling is helping.

And I would like you to take pride in being a salesperson.

I was living an impoverished life until I understood this point well when someone reminded me that I am capable of transforming my life completely to make it bigger, better, and more enriched. I realized that the whole world was actually there to help me, and there were opportunities all around us, if we thought positively.

It's crucial to think positively about Sales, and life will take an upward swing from there.

It's important for a salesperson to keep his thoughts clear and positive. You have to tell a story in your mind – "I know I am helping the customer." Once again, remember this sentence and believe this to your core - "I am helping the customer."

Sales is the process of transferring your confidence, conviction and certainty about your product/ course/ service into the mind of the customer. Only then sales happen. If you believe in the fact that you are helping the customer, you will transfer the positive feeling of certainty to the customer and then it becomes easier to sell.

2. Selling is a compassionate communication

Selling is more than just an emotional exchange. It is a compassionate communication in which you first comprehend the customer's anguish and then assist him overcome it by making an informed decision to purchase. Every pain is resolved with a buying decision. Someone is ill. He buys medicines and gets well. Someone is worried about clearing an examination. He buys some books, a course or joins a coaching centre and gets better at clearing the examination.

Someone buys woollens before visiting a cold country to avoid the pain of suffering from cold in an alien place. Hence, never take sales as a passionate communication where you put in all your energy in convincing the customer to buy. Take it as a compassionate communication where you empathize with problems of the customer and help them take an informed decision to buy the product to make their life better.

Compassion means love, care, understanding others and suggesting them what they need, not what you want to give.

One more point that you need to understand is that sales is nothing but communication. You just need to listen, understand, and develop relationships and sales happen automatically.

3. Selling is always building relationships

A salesperson comes in touch with so many people on a day-to-day basis. He builds networks with new people and we all know our network is our net worth. This is a precious by-product of being in the field of sales. You become the person who knows many and many know him. You become a *walking book* on networking and relationship building.

4. Selling gives you the ability to understand people

Selling gives you a much better understanding of the world than what people in other professions would ever imagine to have. You gain a greater understanding of your relationships, friends, and other members of society. It makes you wise, and as a result, the majority of motivational speakers who teach people the rules of living a happy and successful life originate from the sales industry.

5. Selling is scientific

As you would see in this book – selling is woven around various processes and is not merely about someone's whims and fancies. You will see many formulas and templates on sales in this book, which will make you believe that sales is a science, and not merely an art. Great salespersons are always disciplined and follow the process day in and day out.

6. Selling is an art

While marketing is a science, it is all about understanding people's suffering and needs and creating trust. Hence, it becomes an art as well. It is about observing people and understanding their unique needs. Selling is about understanding people, knowing their pains, connecting with them at a deeper level, showing empathy and coming to help them while building a long-term relationship. It is a great combination of science and art, in fact.

7. Selling is a must-do activity for every organization

Great thing about selling is, it is needed in every organization. An IT services company may not require a factory or warehouse, but it will still need sales professionals. There is a need for sales experts wherever there is competition. Because there is no business or corporation without competition, sales is an essential component of any organization on the planet. This provides salespeople with a diverse set of opportunities.

8. Sales is not about making money. It is about adding value

Money is a result. A sales professional's goal is to add value. As we add value, customers come rushing to us with pay cheques. We can't aim for the pay cheques unless we bring a visible and real value in the life of the customer. If you continue to do what most salespeople do, you will continue to struggle, as many do. You should follow a distinct path in all parts of life, including sales. So instead of speaking only about your products or courses and mentioning their benefits, how about talking about the dreams and goals of the prospect? How about talking about the challenges and difficulties which they are facing? How about talking of their struggles and wins and proposing your products or courses to make that much needed bridge so that they 'cross the otherwise insurmountable river' to their goals on the other end of it?

Once you approach sales from this perspective, you will get undivided attention from the potential customer and chances for their considering buying your product would be high now.

Sales is a journey and as you keep working on more prospects and customers, you keep getting better at it. There will come a time after a few months and years when you will sell without the customer or even you knowing about it. Your conversations and questions will become natural and you will sell in a smooth way.

9. Sales is a great way to support the nation

No nation building activity is possible unless someone sells something to someone else. Be it constructing a bridge, erecting an industrial complex, setting up a chain of colleges, manufacturing a product or delivering a service, sales is always a common factor. Hence, if you sell, you are contributing to the process of country development.

10. 10% sales people in the organization feed the rest 90% people

You will notice a common practice among all corporate; they may or may not have annual operations meetings, but will always have the annual sales meeting, thereby taking sales professionals to some exotic locations and reflecting on the year gone by and planning for the year to come. This is a true reflection of the importance of sales as a function in any organization. Every organization knows internally that they are driven and run by sales people.

So, are you convinced now that sales is good? Everyone must sell.

Every wealthy billionaire is selling. Isn't it interesting that only the middle class, who need the most money, has trouble selling? There are numerous other advantages of selling. If I covered them all, the chapter would be far too long. So, to conclude this chapter, here is my final thought – start selling right now. Because it will allow you and your family to have a better life. PERIOD.

Thequestion now must be, "How do I begin?" So, let's go over this in the following chapters.

And let me ask you this straight:

What's your thinking about sales now?

Do you still feel you must not do it?

I have given you enough reasons by now to learn selling. If you are still not convinced, then you can stop reading this book right here.

But if you are convinced, then move to the next chapter with a rock-solid conviction that you will master this skill at any cost.

Why?

Because this skill is the real insurance of a middle-class family. This is what can give you more money, connects and other things, which you might need any time during your life.

So, let's move to the next chapter with a more positive outlook towards sales.

If you love learning by watching videos, then you may get connected to us for buying the sales course. The details about my team are given on the last page of the book.

Chapter 3
So, are you ready to be a Sales Professional?

Ask this question to yourself before we proceed.

Are you ready to make your first million using this profession called Sales?

I don't want you to become a *Salesman.*

I want you to become a *Sales Professional.*

Sales should be done as a profession and not as a job.

Wondering what is the difference between a 'job' and 'profession'?

It's simple – job earns you a fixed salary whereas a profession earns you a variable amount as per the results.

If you take sales as a job, you will focus on the number of hours you have put in. You won't be driven by the results. In a job, you are not excited for the results as even if you sell more, you will earn the same salary every month. Job will make you tired. You will have to work hard in sales and will have to stay away from your family on quite a few occasions. You will face difficulties and difficulties. If you work in sales, you will not be driven because you will not be compensated for further sales. You will be tired and discouraged soon.

But if you see sales as a profession, you will be habituated to be in a state of energy. You will become accustomed to being in a state of fitness and excellent health because you understand that you must be in the finest possible condition, or else you will miss out on the rewards. You become a lion in a forest which keeps its claws sharp and its body healthy as it knows it has to hunt every now and then. If you are in a job, you are like a lion of a circus. It gets a loaf of meat thrown on its face once or twice a day, and it becomes weak and tired of its life out of boredom. It knows, it will be getting its food thrown in front of it so why to work extra? Anyone who has heard the roar of a lion in a forest knows its intensity and power.

Hence practice sales as a profession to stay in the state of a lifelong learner and earner whose wealth keeps growing in proportion to your energy and fitness. Sales as a profession can give you an ever-increasing scale of growth in money, joys and life which no other profession can even offer. Hence you should work in organizations or institutions where your results as a sales person decides your earnings. Get paid for your results and not for your time and efforts.

Always remember this rule in life – take up sales as a profession and never as a job.

A great sales professional has the following four qualities. Do you have these in you?

Four Qualities (Four Es) of a Sales Professional

As I said, you should come to the field of sales as a professional. A professional is one who does work on his own. He does not need supervision. He is self-driven. He sets tough goals for himself and can move mountains to achieve his goals. He does work without guidance and will find required coaches and mentors to learn from them and seek guidance.

A professional always EDUCATES himself. A person in a job believes that their education is their company's responsibility.

A professional learns from EXPERIENCES. They believe in having the experience of 10,000 hours. Hence, they keep working for ten years with many hours of hard work being put every year. Theyget maximum experience in the shortest possible time. They also try to work for more hours per day so that they complete 10,000 hours in less than ten years.

A professional follows work ETHICS. They keep adding value to the customers on a regular basis. They always take up the calls of customers. Theytreat their customers as god. Theykeep working for giving new and value adding experience to customers. They never leave their customers, even after giving values. You must set and follow some values as a salesperson. Ethics and values are must for any good sales person.

I have created sales courses for people who are in a state-of-the-art Learning Management System. I always believe in giving the best value through my courses. My goal is to give the kind of content and value which no other competitor can give. Hence, my eLearning courses are at par with the best. I have told my team to give the best value and customer service to my customers. If my customers are not happy, my team has a strict instruction to refund their money with utmost respect and care. However, my customers also know that once they purchase a product or service from me, they are 100% sure to get the best content. Theywould be getting the quality and service which

I had promised to them. Theywould be getting more than what they had been promised for. That is the kind of work ethic which makes a great salesperson.

A professional is always ready for EXAMINATION. He is prepared to be scrutinised by the client by assisting the consumer in times of need. He is prepared to take exams until he is successful.

How can you earn millions using Sales?

Let's take a couple of examples.

In the first example, we have a real estate salesperson who wants to make a million. If he sells three properties worth Rs 2 crore, he can make Rs 6 lakh in a day. Now how much effort he needs to put?

He needs to advertise in his circle.

He needs to show the property to at least five people, three times each. So, fifteen visits mean fifteen hours. He might need to help in the registration process.

So, to put together, he spends around fifty hours – 100 hours to earn Rs 6,00,000 which will take around a year or 2400 hours of efforts for a salaried person.

I have a friend, Surender Vats. He is a professional Network Marketer. He has been associated with RCM business for the last twenty-three years. Today, he has a popular YouTube channel named – 'Chat With Surender Vats'. You may follow him. You know what! Every month he generates INR 100 crore + worth of business for his company and he is a Crown Diamond in his organization. He certainly does it through a big team but he himself, with his hard work and incredible selling skill, has built this wonderful team. Isn't it amazing? It's fantastic for sure.

Let me take the example of a trainer. Suppose the trainer has a moderate experience of five years in the field. Even then he can charge Rs 50,000 per session. By conducting two sessions per week, he can earn Rs 4,00,000 per month which you earn in a job only when you spend at least twenty-five years. Hence, even by a conservative calculation, a trainer with five years of experience earns more than a salaried person of twenty-five years! If we take the example of an experienced trainer who, say, has an experience of 10-15 years, he can easily charge 3-5 lakh per workshop. By conducting eight programmes per month, he can earn Rs 40,00,000 which is equal to the salary of 4-6 Managing Directors' salary in India! To cite my example, I have earned more than Rs 40,00,000 in just one hour as well.

Let's have a fresh perspective on Sales

Assume you offer your friend Rs 10 lakh and he does not repay your money on time. You will contact him. You will continue to visit his home until you receive your money from that pal.

Now let's imagine – your Rs 10 crore is with people. And you just need to make calls. You need to send an SMS and contact people over WhatsApp. You need to build relations and recover your money.

Hence, selling is recovering your money which is kept with other people.

Hence, fortune is in follow-up.

Follow-up in sales is something you should remember for the rest of your life.

I need a commitment from you.

So, do you understand why sales is important?

Now, are you clear that sales is the best thing in the world?

Earl Nightingale says, "The biggest problem of the world is that people do not actually think."

I welcome you to the field which gave me everything I wanted. It gave me the power to help transform the lives of millions of people and it also gave me the power to achieve my own goals of joys, wealth, fulfilment and adding value to others. If you know me and have chosen to read this book, it's because of this field which I had decided to master many years ago. A salesperson is independent in life and can earn any amount of money they want.

Visualize a situation: You go to a businessman and tell him that you are a salesperson. You confidently say, with a smile on your face, that you can sell a record amount of his products and services within a record short time at the highest possible margin and he in turn will pay the commission. You can easily imagine a gleam in the businessman's eyes. You suddenly become a highly valued individual, who is in high demand. You will undoubtedly receive preferential treatment as a result of your interaction with the businessman. After all, who in this world does not want to sell his products and services?

Any businessman or person in authority rose to this position through his ability to sell, and they always value a competent salesperson. This is one profession which is valued in every domain of life; and one who can sell can surely rise to the top in any business or organization. A research data shows that 90% CEOs in corporates are from sales background. Which goes to say that they have worked as sales person at some point of time in their career. The Board trusts such people with the responsibility of running the company.

A businessman values people who can sell his products and services and make customers pay in a win-win way. Those who do not know sales, will struggle all their life; and those who know sales are the absolute winners in life. People who have good knowledge of sales get high returns for their efforts and are the wealthiest of people. In corporate, sales people are paid the highest salary and increments. They are invited to beautiful national and international locations to celebrate and be a part of annual sales meets. On the other hand, those who are not in sales keep wondering why they do not get the special treatments as their sales colleagues receive!

Sales is one skill which can make you a multi-millionaire, but only *when you love sales*. Sales means rejection and you can handle rejection while still moving on, only if you love sales. If you don't love sales, you can't be rich. No organization has ever grown without sales. No entity has ever expanded without sales, whether it is a corporation, a business, or a religious institution. Whether you visit Patanjali, Isha Yoga, or the Art of Living Foundation, you will find them 'selling' their programmes to you. Though their intention is to see you transform your life, they will still sell their courses to you. Unless they sell their courses to you and make you buy, you won't get any benefit from your visit to their centres or websites. Lives change and the companies become great only if they sell their products and services.

When you begin to learn sales, you will be welcomed by rejections, and some more rejections. You have to be ready for rejections. It's not an easy and smooth experience and this explains why there are so few sales professionals in a world which is addicted to being in the comfort zone. How can you fall in love with sales? You can do so only if you visualize the benefits of sales. You need to write down all the goals and dreams of your life. Then you need to write in big bold letters – 'All my dreams will come true if I master the skill of selling.'

You should spend at least two hours while writing all your dreams and goals. Take some old magazines and cut down the pictures of things which represent your goals. Then paste the picture of all your goals on a Vision Board. You need to internalize the feeling that you will attain all the goals which you have displayed on the Vision Board, if you just learn the skill of sales. The more time you spend while writing down and sketching your goals and correlating this with the skill of sales, the easier it will become for you to handle rejections and learn and master sales as a skill.

All of my dreams have come true solely because of one skill – sales. I drive expensive cars and live in opulent mansions. I go to exotic locations and meet some of the world's most powerful people. I take my family to some of the most sought-after hotels and holiday destinations and the secret lies in one skill – my selling skills. Be it a coach or shopkeeper, the one who does not sell will live an obscure life.

The last thing before we begin the process

Before the process, realize that sales is the only profession which can give you as much money as you want.

You can learn the skill.

You can master it.

You just need to follow the process as depicted in the remainder of the book.

Ready to go?

Flip through the pages ahead…

Chapter 4
Getting Ready – Habits of a good Sales Professional

Let's start from the beginning of the process.

First of all, you need to get deeper into your products and services. You need to know their every aspect. 'Eat, drink and sleep' your products and services and master them in and out. Take a few days off if necessary, and spend as many hours as possible studying the product and learning its features by reading manuals, speaking with product experts, and learning about its segments and customers. Spend time while writing down the benefits of products, and the changes it can bring in the life of customers. Be the best person in the world on your products and services. That is the first requirement.

After you are done with this (and it might take a few days or weeks), get mentally prepared for the sales work. Now it's the transition from knowing your products in and out to convincing customers about why the product is the most suited for them.

The next logical step is, building powerful habits. You must build these habits to be great in this field:

- **Read books:** Reading books is one tool every company, where selling is the key, recommends. Read the book by experts who have spent many decades studying deeper into a particular topic. You will find many books on a diverse range of topics, including sales, peak performance, emotional intelligence, art of negotiation, etc. Reading a book is like spending a few hours of undiluted time with the best experts in the field. You can get the secrets of success in just a few hours, which the author might have gained in decades. Hence, always say yes to the habit of reading books.
- **Meditate:** A salesperson must practice meditation. This can be done for 3 minutes, 5 minutes, 15 minutes, or longer. Take whatever time you need, but meditation is required on a daily basis. As a salesperson, you will come across many situations that can lead to stress. Some days will be full of wins and others will have misses. Meditation helps you keep your energy focused. There are moments when I get to know just before a conference that the hall is only 40% full. Initially, while planning for the show, we had expected a packed hall. Now what do you do? Just take a deep breath and smile while thinking – "Let him see. He has brought me thus far in life. He will also see me ahead." This one thought will change the pattern of thinking in a positive direction and you will do great even in an

unpacked hall. This always works. Then you say – "Today is your day. Come in the state of flow. Make it your best day. Transform the lives of people." I have seen the journey in life from 20% packed halls to 150% packed halls. It's a journey; and with spirituality, it all becomes easier.

- **Affirmations:** Sales means focusing on yourself and your goals. Stop watching movies of other superstars. Say to yourself – "You are the superstar". If other superstars cannot leave their jobs for you, why should you abandon your priorities and job? A salesperson should develop a razor-sharp focus on his goals and skills. You must write down a set of affirmations and say them every day, preferably in the morning hours. Some of these affirmations could be as follows:

I am the best salesperson who can sell to anyone

I sell to help others

I sell to make the world bigger

I am the best

Sales is the best profession

I am proud to be a salesperson

I am the most powerful resource person for my customers

I am a champion of sales

Write your own affirmations and practice them every day to build a robust mindset which never accepts defeat against rejections.

- **Focus on each customer:** You never know which customer will bring you millions of dollars worth of business. For you he might be the hundredth customer, but for him, you might be the first person from the organization/seller he is speaking with. Hence, please make it a habit to focus on each customer. Of course, we are speaking about the customers who are from your target segments.
- **Gratitude:** You are going to practice gratitude; you should be thankful to god and destiny. The great philosopher Marcus Tullius Cicero said, "Gratitude is not only the greatest of virtues, but the parent of all the others." You can practice gratitude and write a few sentences in your diary or say these every day in the morning.
    - Thank you god for the beautiful family, which supports me even when the world may turn its back on me
    - I know for sure that there are millions of people in this world who do not have a family to support them.
    - Thank you god for the ability to read, write and speak. I know for sure that there are millions of people in this world who can't speak, read or write and suffer lots of problems in life. I am so blessed to have these abilities, which make my life so beautiful.
    - Thank you so much god for those people who have uploaded life transformational learning videos, podcasts and audiobooks by listening to which I can learn new lessons of

life and profession, while being at any place at any point of time.

- Thank you so much god for the appreciation, which I received from my peers for my fast reply to their queries. Millions are living their life without hearing a word of appreciation.

Gratitude is something that should be done every day, ideally in the early morning hours!

- Set Goals: Sales runs on target setting. Unless you set targets, you can't sell. In corporations, annual sales meetings are held during which targets are given to sales heads. Once you set targets, be ruthless to attain them. I have always set targets to attain sales. Without targets, forget about the aspiration to become a great salesperson. I have always been setting targets for myself. I set a target of buying Mercedes Benz, resort, house and publishing books. I set targets for selling my programmes worth crores. I have always been running for these targets. I have set a target to inspire 50 crore people. Hence, I have set a target to earn 100 crores, as there is a huge cost involved in marketing and spreading my reach. There is a huge cost involved in holding events, be it an online event or a physical conference. Whatever the way, set targets and break records. Do not break yourself in return. If you set goals and stick to them as if your life depended on it, you will undoubtedly smash records. Build networks and affiliations, travel, take out loans if necessary, form a team – whatever it takes, set goals and pursue them. In every company, they set annual and monthly sales targets and cascade it down to every sales person's key result areas. This is just an example of how important target setting is in the field of sales.

- Self-Review: You must have the discipline of reviewing yourself every day. You must review your performance against the targets and whether you are adding value to yourself. Things which do not get reviewed will never get done. It needs discipline and is more difficult than setting goals, as it needs repetitive actions.
- Discipline: Sales is about having a standard routine and following a set pattern of actions every day.
    - You have to make many calls every day.
    - You must follow up with the customers every day.
    - You have to meet new customers every day.
    - You have to update your sales tracker or record every day.
    - You have to face rejections every day.

Now the question is – will it not be boring? Yes, it will be, if you do not see the results and/or if you are not making progress or self-development every day. Such a situation will lead to frustration. Hence, your goal should be in front of your eyes. Please make your Vision Board and display it on the wall. If you have not made it, you may take up one of my e-learning courses and make it. I conduct a programme called 'Discover Your Vision' both online and offline. You should see it every day. Write down a set of affirmations and read it out aloud every day. These are the ways to train your sub-conscious mind for success. Do not underestimate the power of your thoughts. To share my experience, I see that 80% of things which I depict on the Vision Board get done automatically.

By taking some of the actions mentioned above, you can convert taking the set pattern of actions into something enjoyable.

- **Keep the tracker:** Whether you use an excel sheet or a whiteboard, you must keep a tracker. Review your performance and enter it into the tracker. Use different colours to make the tracker even more value adding and helpful.

As the next step, you must have a process of maintaining and reviewing your Sales report. A typical sales report (you can maintain it in an MS Excel or in any other format convenient to you) should have the following:

Suspect: A suspect is a company or individual that fits the right client profile but may not:

- Be actively looking for your product or service
- Have needs that your product or service can address
- Be in a position to purchase for one reason or another
- Have been properly qualified
- Get you to the right people that can help with decision making or make a decision

Prospect: A prospect is a company or individual with a known need for your product or service and who you've already qualified.

Pipeline: A sales pipeline is an organized, visual way of tracking potential buyers as they progress through different stages in the purchasing process and buyer's journey. Often, pipelines are visualized as a horizontal bar, sometimes as a funnel, divided into the various stages of a company's sales process. If you have a sale of 5 crore INR in pipeline, then you can be sure that you will keep getting around 1 crore every month just by following-up and by maturing these customers.

Hence Sales pipeline report must be maintained and this must keep on growing every month on month.

Closing report: It's a report mentioning the closing of sales made and this can be maintained on daily or weekly basis.

Day sales report: Earlier, we have discussed the importance of setting goals in Sales. We also discussed how sales is all about setting annual goals and then breaking them into quarterly, monthly, weekly and daily goals. Unless goals are broken down in this manner, you will never be inspired to take daily and consistent actions, and hence sales will not happen. Any good salesperson knows the power of target setting and following-up.

We just spoke about following-up. Do you think we can follow-up effectively against the actual execution if we do not create a MIS or report which is easy to comprehend and use? Obviously, it's not possible.

Here comes the significance of reporting. You have got to use a reporting format (MS Excel, etc.) in which you keep a track of the following on daily basis:

1. Number of suspects contacted
2. Number of prospects
3. Sales made
4. Follow-up with old prospects to create sales pipeline

I rank the last point as a crucial one. Let me explain why.

While it's important to make and report sales, it's equally or even more important to follow-up with old prospects or else you will not create a sales pipeline.

Take the reporting to the next level by marking the prospects as 'Super-Hot', 'Hot', 'Warm' and 'Cold'. You can do this with colour coding. For example, in case you are using an excel sheet, use red, orange, yellow and blue to indicate each type of prospects, respectively.

Segmentation of people: This is done among a range, including super-hot, hot, warm, lukewarm, cold and dead. Accordingly, we need to colour code the customers. Prospecting can be done in two ways – direct and indirect. First of all, not everyone can be called a prospect. A prospect is someone who I recommend to people to do indirect prospecting, which is about building relationships.

In direct prospecting, you try selling your products in direct terms which many people do not like. Nobody wants to be sold. They do want to buy, which means thereby they like making their own decisions. Hence, when you meet people, trying generating curiosity in their mind about the kind of work you do and the product or service which you offer.

For instance, when you meet a person, begin by saying something about yourself which will make them curious about you and your products. Then, you can tell them about your products in a manner that they can connect the products with their business and see for themselves how its going to help them. As you start enlisting prospects, you need to know the categories of prospects. Not every prospect has the same degree of readiness for buying your products. There are six different types of prospects:

1. Super-hot: These prospects agree with all your ideas. They ask you relevant questions with the intention to know more and take notes. They appear to be interested in what you teach and offer. Theyhave the funds and time to purchase your items and courses. Theyare linked to you and participate in all of your programmes. They are quite likely to purchase from you.
2. Hot: These prospects ask questions and take notes. They are interested, but may not be immediately ready to purchase from you. With little interaction and sorting of queries, they will join your programme.
3. Warm: Theyare positive participants and are likely to come after some time. They are connected with you meanwhile.
4. Lukewarm: Not sure whether they are open or not. Keep them connected through emails, etc.
5. Cold: No interaction or sharing of ideas. No questions. May be, just may be, they will become warm with a change in their life situations. They may have some situations or challenges later in life and may be driven towards you. For now, they are silent.
6. Dead: Name spells it all.

Practice Sales – practice makes perfect!

Many people enter the field of sales, but never practice it. A salesperson must practice for years, much like a musician or a sportsperson does for years and decades. My experience says that one has to practice sales for around 7-8 years before you can start earning 1-2 crores per month. However, you should not feel demotivated while looking at the long timeframe which I mentioned. You will start earning a lakh or two per month from the very first year. It needs consistency on daily basis, though. I have a few team members who earn lakhs of rupees per month and have increased their earnings to millions of rupees in only a few months, all because of this one ability of selling. Practice makes a person perfect and this is true with sales as well. You should be ready to practice for many years and it has to be done every day. Returns will be huge and rewarding. Isn't it reason enough to grasp the art and science of selling?

Magical Sales Mantra

Here, I am going to share two mantras with you, which you must follow on daily basis.

These mantras are: OVERCOMMIT and OVERDELIVER.

Though these are applicable in business as well, but in Sales, it's a must. Yes, you must overcommit and overdeliver if you want to be a great salesperson.

When I was to create and launch an e-Learning programme, I committed to the customers that I will be giving a hundred videos, which was purely a case of overcommitment. Let me explain how.

I have never seen any other coach or content creator delivering a sales programme with as many as a hundred videos. The creation, editing, and posting of these numerous videos will undoubtedly be a major undertaking that will require a significant amount of time and effort. I needed to create videos on as many sub-topics under just one heading – Sales.

In addition, I needed to add the e-Learning courses on Network Marketing, Telephone Marketing and Commando Training, at no extra cost at all. This bundle of four courses would make this one master course of Sales, one of the most powerful courses in the country.

And then I overdelivered on all these programmes. I worked harder than any other person could and then delivered all these programmes ahead of time and at an impeccable quality. That is what the customers love. This is a basic rule of Sales – overcommit and overdeliver.

Many people think the other way – they want people to under-commit and overdeliver. No, this is not a good idea. If you overcommit, you stretch the powers of your mind and body and do what you would never have done, had you under-committed.

Whenever you are discussing with the customer, give him two overcommitments. For example, you can tell the customer – sir, I will give you free service for lifetime. I will call back on the same day. And then you keep your word. That is the spirit of a salesperson which makes them one of the richest in the world.

If you get these two tenets of Sales, you will experience a remarkable transformation in the way you have been leading your life. Your whole personality will change and that is the essence of being a winning salesperson.

Chapter 5
Sales as a Science – Sales Processes for assured results!

In this chapter, we will look at some of the most important sales processes. By learning these sales techniques, anyone can become a great sales professional. Let's look at some of the crucial sales processes.

Sales and the importance of SWOT analysis

You must do the SWOT analysis to sell well.

In Sales, result equals money. People often complain that they are not able to produce results despite taking years. I say that bringing results takes lesser time than not bringing out the results. People waste years while not learning new skills and not doing the needful to develop their powers to bring out results.

Let me bring more clarity here.

People have to do their SWOT analysis. Theyhave to understand their strengths, weaknesses, opportunities and threats. While strengths and weaknesses are internal factors, opportunities and threats are external and come from the surrounding. Some people, whose strength lies in the field of online sales, do physical sales. The vice versa is also true. People can have many weaknesses:

Their pronunciation is not good.

Their vocabulary is not good.

They do not have dressing etiquette.

Individuals must be self-aware. This will result from self-observation. Sell while watching your recorded footage. Then view other sales experts' recorded videos. Make a comparison and suggestions for improvement. Draw a circle and divide it into four parts. Write your strengths, weaknesses, opportunities and threats in each of the segments and meditate over these.

For those readers who want to learn the skill of sales, one of the most effective ways is to be a part of my 'learn and earn' scheme, about which you can take more information from my team.

Customer Approach Techniques

There are four stages in Sales Approach – Opening, Probing, Closing and Supporting.

The first stage, i.e. Opening is only for grabbing the attention of customers. To cite an example, if you are creating a YouTube video, you need to grab the attention of the customer in the first three seconds. It's a very short attention span nowadays indeed and if you are not able to grab the attention of the customer early, chances are very high that the customer will not even watch the remainder of the video even if it has a strong message or content. That is the power of '**Opening**'.

Your opening remark or pitch has to be strong. This is true for both, online meetings, and offline.

Then comes the stage of **Probing**. In this stage, you ask the customers what their challenges are. You start talking about the pain of the customer and suggest your solutions or the features of your products which can help him. For example, if you are the salesperson of a wall painting company, you start talking about the condition of paint on the walls of his house. You mention issues with worn out paint or chipping paint in specific spots. You begin discussing the issues and engage the customer in conversation. The customer begins to gravitate towards your items or services at this point. In the third stage of **Closing**, you close the sales; meaning thereby the customer signs the agreement and pays money. You give him the products and services. There are eleven sub-stages under Closing, which we will discuss in the chapters to come.

Fourth stage of sales is **Supporting** the customers and keeping your promises which were made in the course of selling. You have to support the customer well so that he becomes your brand ambassador and gives business in a repeat mode. He will also tell others about you and will indirectly become the reason for growing your business.

Let's Learn About Sales Ketting: 3 stages

If you have seen my sales webinars, you might recall that I had told you about the kind of dream life which you want to live. When someone else is talking about your dreams and is talking about the ways to make it a reality for you, you begin to feel a connection with the individual. Let me take a few examples. A salesperson for AC must demonstrate the dream of sleeping in cosy pleasures. He will ask you to imagine a situation in which you sleep comfortably even in a city known for scorching heat in summer. He will ask you to imagine the happiness on the face of your family members when they wake up in the morning and feel happy while saying thank you to you for having got a nice AC at home. He is selling you a dream before you dig into your wallet to pay thousands of rupees to have the AC installed in your bedroom.

Another example – suppose a salesperson is selling you a retirement plan. He can bring your attention to those few months during Covid-19 when people suffered due to lack of work and money. Then he will tell you how you would survive after your retirement for so many years. When people suffered for just a few months, it was terrible. Then, what kind of problem people may land in if they have to spend decades after their retirement? Now he is selling you a dream. By just spending a little money, you can secure your life post-retirement.

Sales ketting is one tool which you must keep in mind while selling your products and services. Customers don't buy your products or services; they buy dreams.

Additionally, you have to build a brand while spreading word about you, your products, and your company. Share stories about satisfied customers talking about your products. For example, while selling an LED light, you can talk about the savings of Rs 50,000 in a year. Initial cost is high, but overall cost savings would be significant. You can use this amount to purchase a laptop for your child. You can also bear the school fees for your children. This is the product which is saving these many units of electricity. Talk about the competitors' LED bulbs and the superior performance of your products. Talk about your credentials. Talk about the certification from various agencies and good word of mouth. Talk about positive reports of the research and the positive results that your customers have received.

Then create a buzz while talking about the scarcity of the product. Tell people about the limited availability of the product. You can tell them that the product is selling fast and is getting out of stock. It's better for the customers to buy the product today itself. The demand is so high that we are not able to maintain any stock. Products are sold as soon as the new stock arrives. If you do not place the order now, you will not have any stocks left. You can purchase the products now. We will give you a discount of 15% if you purchase it now. You will get additional benefit, which is a free service for the next one year. This one-year service would normally cost you five thousand rupees which is absolutely free for you.

So, to summarize, Sales Ketting has three dimensions:

Selling a dream

Building brand, and

Creating buzz

Sales follows the Law of averages

Many people say that they are not getting results in sales. I say – people always get results. Some consumers will buy your products, regardless of how lousy a salesperson you are. Even the finest salesperson cannot sell 100% of the products and services. If there are 2000 people in my webinar, at least 10-12% people will surely buy the courses.

Efforts and improvisation must go hand in hand. Keep taking actions and enhance the efforts, if needed. Suppose you want to earn Rs 1 lakh and you are making a hundred calls. If you have earned only Rs 70,000, you have to enhance the number of calls. You also need to work on reducing time for making each call. Also, you can improvise on your closing rate.

Hence efforts, improvisations and calculations – keep doing these to get results. You are bound to get results. Do not lose heart.

You must love *targets* if you are in Sales

Sales runs on target setting. Unless you set targets, you can't sell.

In corporations, annual sales meetings are held in which targets are given to sales heads.

Once you've defined your goals, you must be ruthless in order to achieve them. I have always set targets to attain sales. Without targets, forget about the aspiration to become a great salesperson. I have always been setting targets for me. I set a target of buying Mercedes Benz, resort, house and publishing books. I set targets for selling my programmes worth crores. I have always been running for these targets. I have a target to inspire fifty crore people. Hence, I have set a target to earn 100 crores as there is a huge cost involved in marketing and spreading my reach. There is huge cost involved in holding events, be it an online event or a physical conference.

Whatever be the way, set targets and break records. Do not get broken in return. If you keep targets and follow them as if your life depends on them, you will surely be a record breaker. Build networks and associations, travel, take loan if needed, build a team – do whatever you have to do, but set targets and go after them. In every company, they set annual and monthly sales targets and cascade it down to every sales person's key result areas. This is just an example of how important target setting is in the field of sales.

Become a Pro at Value Creation

Sales is like a vehicle which runs on two wheels – one is target and second is value creation. Just setting targets will not help you if you do not add or create value in the life of customers. You must develop yourself so that you start adding some kind of value in others' life.

Let's take the example of automobiles. You have so many cars in the market that it's so easy to get confused. You have Indian, Japanese, German and European cars in the market. Each car maker has multiple brands in the market. Each brand of car has different features. If the sales person does not help the customer in making a buying decision, the customer will get confused as there are multiple varieties of products which serve the same broad purpose, but as you go deeper, each brand has something unique. These second level unique features are often not that obvious and hence a good sales person knows how to understand the specific budget, requirements and preferences of the customer and suggest the type of car which is the best for the customer.

I have been in the field of selling since more than a decade. I have seen my life being transformed from a naïve buyer to a confident seller. I always take queries from customers to understand their needs first. I will never open all the products to the customers in the beginning. First, I will understand his preference and the budget and will then propose only that programme which meets the need. Once I have closed the sale of one programme which adds value in the life of the customer, I will open discussion on other programmes to tell them what else is there to add value to them. Customers may buy some of these programmes now or in future. This is how you close a sale and also plan future sale.

If you propose all products at the same time, you are making the customer overwhelmed and confused, which will not make the sale happen. Customer will remain unsatisfied as his need is not met. You become frustrated as your sale did not happen. Remember, the universe grows only when someone in some corner of the world makes a sale.

Remember what would have happened if Elon Musk would not have made a sale to NASA.

What would have happened if Jeff Bezos did not make a sale of books in 1990s to customers. Amazon Web Services and other companies would not have existed.

What would have happened if Mark Zuckerberg had not made a sale of his idea of social connectedness to the investors. Millions of people who get healthier while seeing the daily Facebook live yoga talks of Swami Ramdev would not have been benefitted on the health front. I conduct so many Facebook live sessions and get connected with millions of people every month. It's only because I could sell and connect with a larger audience.

This is the power of closing a deal. Value creation is at the core of sales. All the people mentioned in the above paragraphs have mastered the art and science of value creation.

You create value and then the sale happens.

Here, we also need to understand one more point. You cannot keep meeting the customer only for selling something, or else they will get bored. Here, I need to share the SPANCOP model for you. It's there on my YouTube channel. You must watch this video. In a nutshell, let me give an idea of how the SPANCOP process works.

SPANCOP is an acronym which stands for the following:

Suspect: Identification of potential opportunities within your target segment.

Prospect: Qualify the opportunities and establish your prospects' list.

Analyze and Approach: Determine the needs and establish genuine interest. Analyze the prospects and mark them as 'Superhot', 'Hot', 'Warm' and 'Cold'.

Negotiate: This stage involves negotiation with the clients on the pricing aspect of the deal and its associated terms and conditions. During this stage, you should demonstrate that the value of your product exceeds the price the buyer is willing to pay.

Close: At this point of the sales cycle, the client would agree to the terms and conditions of the deal or contract. The deal would be considered to be "Closed", when the customer would sign on the contract and would complete all the necessary formalities for issuing a purchase order to you.

Order: This is the last stage of the sales cycle, wherein the client would issue the Purchase Order (PO) and order fulfilment is done. Once a PO is issued, the salesperson has to hand it over to the concerned Operations Department or Fulfilment or Delivery Team, which would carry it forward. The client's responsibility is transferred to the Delivery Team. This marks the end of the sales cycle for that particular deal.

Payment: Here we refer to the actual receipt of payment, as sales are never complete unless you receive the money.

Being genuinely connected to the customers and adding psychological value is equally important. I have been conducting free 'Think Rich' shows through which lakhs of people are connecting with me. They are getting some value out of my free talks and feel good. This is a good example of adding value in a subtle way at a psychological level. You can also add value while looking at someone's social media post and making a genuine and creative comment. For example, you can wish someone on his/her birthday in a genuine and creative way. You can spend some time while checking people's feeds and choose to make some heart-warming comments which should be made with genuine interest to make someone happy. These are the ways of value creation without spending any money, but these have a strong impact on your relationship with customers.

I will strongly suggest that you spend one dedicated hour on social media every day not watching reels for the sake of fun, but watching important updates from people who matter the most to you and making some genuine comments and wishing them in a special way. You can send some personalized message to people on their special occasions.

Product Stacking, a Grand Way to Scale Your Sales Potential

I have watched many people in the field of sales and have observed one thing – They work in companies which depend on just one product. This is a mistake you should never make. Work in companies which have a stack of multiple products. I have been earning an average of Rs 80 lakhs to 1 crore every month and people wonder how we are able to do this. I always say that the biggest secret for our consistently good performance is our creation and selling of multiple products. I have a wide range of products, including Sales Brahmastra, Memory Enhancement Technique, Discover Your Vision, Commando

Training, Book Writing programme, Business Coaching, One to One Coaching, Stock Market Mastery, Public Speaking and many other products and training programmes. These programmes serve a wide range of audience and some of these products keep selling across the year.

You take the example of Apple. People mostly know this company for iPhones, but is it the end of product range for Apple? Not at all. Theyhave Macbook, iPad, AirPods and other such products. Amazon also has Amazon Web Services, Prime Video and other products. I am not advising you to be in products which are not related to the field of your core competence, but always keep a range of products across various cost and quality. Only then you can cater to a large number of customers. Going back to the example of Apple, the company has maintained a wide range of iPhones, starting from a low to a high price range, to cater to the needs of every segment of their target customers. This simply distributes your risk and allows you to keep selling in every season and market conditions to various customer groups.

Product stacking is an important aspect of selling.

The Simple, Yet The Most Powerful Formula of 3333

You must follow the formula 3333 in the field of sales. What does it mean?

Here is the explanation.

You start with making **3 calls** every day to new customers and do this for a month. When I say three calls, that means speaking to three customers and being able to connect with them in a deeper way. This doesn't mean that you actually make only 3 calls. You might need to make thirty calls, but three must be super productive calls where you can say that these are my 'hot' or 'super-hot' customers.

Next month onwards, you start sending **3 proposals** everyday to some of these customers you have called in the last month. While doing so, you continue making three calls every day. So, by the end of the second month, you have made 180 calls and sent ninety proposals.

Then after another month, make **3 follow-ups** every day. At the end of three months, you have made 270 calls, have sent 180 proposals and have made ninety follow-ups.

After the end of **3 months**, now you are in the fourth month. You start closing 3 Sales every week. This is in the backdrop of corporate, where holding even three meetings in a day would be a great achievement. At the end of four months, you have made 360 calls, have sent 270 proposals, have made 180 follow-ups and have held ninety closings.

This is the rule of thumb for an average business. If you want to increase the sales, you can start making 4-5 productive calls every day instead of making just three calls.

Now you have got the point, I am sure 😊.

This is the Sales Formula 3333.

Put it to use. Remember that sales requires dedication and that the fortune is in the follow-ups. As a result of constantly chatting to potential customers and keeping track of follow-ups, victory will be on your side.

Sales and the ways to find customers

The easiest way to start the process of sales is to begin with soft targets. Now the question is – who are the soft targets? These are as follows:

Friends: These are your friends who will not refuse your request to buy a product or programme. Your true friends will always want to support you. If you have confidence in your product, reach out to your friends.

Family: Apart from friends, you should reach out to your family. Yes, this allows you to softly practice your selling talents, and they are micro acts or small steps that prepare you to sell to strangers. Later on, as you develop your community, you will not need any help from your family and friends.

Neighbours: I know it may not be easy to reach out to neighbours, but they could also be your customers. The idea is to have confidence in your products or services and reach out to people, who you never know, could be looking for these products and may lap your products. This is a short-term strategy, as later on, you will be reaching out to a large number of external people, but initially the soft targets do help you grow.

Every Professional Salesperson and Organization build Sales Funnels

One of the key concepts of sales is to design a funnel. This is my favourite too, as this can help you generate a lot of money. So, let's understand in simple terms what a sales funnel is.

You might be having many products and services to sell to a wide range of customers, but each customer has different sets of needs and you also have a variety of products for a range of prices, providing various benefits. You need to first let customers experience you, your company and your broad range of offering. The customer is new to you, or we can also say, you are new to the customers. Hence, you should keep a free or very low-cost product which customers will not mind just giving a try. Once the customers come to your contact and experience your products and services, it's an opportunity for you to let customers know about other high value products. Let your customers spend some time with you, and then only they will build some basic level of trust. As you all know, building trust takes time and unless the customer has faith on you, he or she will not begin buying high value products or services from you.

Now, are you getting a sense of what a sales funnel is? Let's get more clarity.

It's a funnel in which you invite customers to build trust on you, your ability and your products and then customers try buying some low cost and low engagement programmes. Gradually, they will trust you more and find it easy to buy more products with higher stakes, which might cost them higher. As you keep inducting more customers in your funnel, more and more customers go on buying your products of various types and your market bases expand. Also, you get more referrals from an ever-increasing customer base; use these referrals to attract new customers.

This is how a funnel keeps attracting a larger base at the top of it (refer to the diagram below). As you go down the funnel, you find higher value programmes.

In the diagram given below, you can see my free programmes like 'The Magic of Thinking Rich' at the top whereas my costliest programme 'Business Tycoon Manufacturing Process' at the bottom.

The price range starts with nothing and moves down to seven to ten lakh rupees.

In between, I have a wide range of programmes which, by now, are hundreds in numbers.

A sales funnel allows me to cater to customers with various problems, looking for specific solutions.

If a customer is looking for some basic motivation and direction in life, he or she can come for 'Magic of Thinking Rich'. Number of such customers goes in millions and crores in my case.

Some of these audience members are looking for a programme on how to build better 'English Speaking' courses. They buy my programmes on 'Spoken English' and 'Public speaking'. A few others may opt for my programme 'Commando Training' to build higher energy, focus and power. Others may buy a programme on Selling Skills, Stock Trading or various other programmes. I have been in the field of training, breakthrough strategy and business transformation for more than fifteen years and have more than 100 such programmes to offer.

I am sure after having a cursory look at the diagram given below, you would have understood what sales funnel is and how crucial it is for your success as a sales professional.

To take the example of a coding trainer, he has to keep a stack of products including basic courses on coding as well as advance coding certification programmes. In between, he can have software language training courses which may range from free to low to mid to high ticket courses.

The basics of sales funnel are the following:

- You need an assortment of products or courses.
- You need courses across a range of price points.

- You need to stack the products in such a manner that customers gradually buy upgraded courses.
- You need to expand the community base and educate them gradually, so that they are aware of your offerings and purchase various courses of high prices as they build more trust on you and your credentials.

Let's take another example of a writing coach. His product portfolio can include free blogs which he can do every day to let people know that he is there in this field. He can have multiple products of different price points including the following:

- Writing books for others (high ticket product)
- Doing copy writing work (low ticket product)
- Mentoring budding authors to complete their book (mid ticket product)
- Mentoring budding authors to write a book and build their author's brand (high ticket product)
- Mentoring budding authors to write and publish eBooks (low ticket product)
- Conducting talks in corporates, institutions and colleges on 'how to become an author' (low to mid ticket product)

Creating a stack of products helps the coach in launching his lowest ticket course to introduce himself to customers, some of whom may buy high ticket courses or products later on. He needs to develop his sales funnel.

To take the example of a sports trainer, he can have multiple products of different price points, including the following:

- Giving free talks in colleges to let them know about the importance of sports and also to make them aware of his capabilities.
- He can take batches of students and train them in sports.
- He can provide personal training to sports enthusiasts.
- He can write blogs on sports.
- He can interview sports personalities to enhance his brand image and grow his community.
- He can launch a range of sports accessories and products which could be in low to high budget range.
- He can provide sports training to corporates which could be a high ticket offering, etc.

We can have multiple examples, but basically, a Sales Funnel consists of three different types of products/services:

- Top of the funnel: Here, you stack your offerings which are basically to spread awareness and discovery.
- Middle of the funnel: Here, you stack products which are higher in value and price and the customers need some research backed data to be able to make the buying decisions.
- Bottom of the funnel: This is the basket of the costliest products and services which require an educated buying decision.

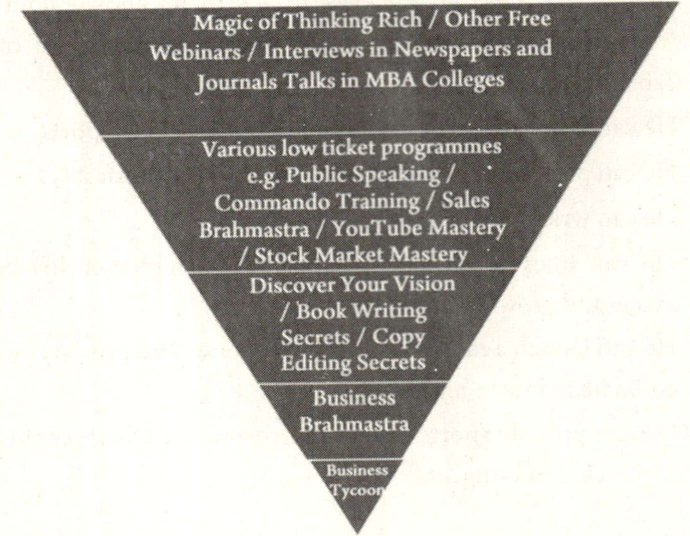

You must understand the concept of sales funnel and hence I give you some more examples and details around this.

Let's start with an example. You go to a restaurant and order some chapatti/bread and vegetables. It's a basic meal which you are ordering, but the waiter may also ask whether you would like to have some *masala papad* or soup. You will also find some displays mentioning special offers in a particular timeframe. The waiter may also tell you about the offer being given that evening. He may also offer you some desserts.

It all started from just chapatti and sabji, and moved on to many other dishes.

So, what is sales funnel?

Let's take the example of a motivational trainer who offers courses to meet various improvement needs of customers. He creates a funnel of products so that initially, he offers low cost products or courses to customers who do not know him well. After the customers have taken that course and have got a good degree of trust about the trainer, they will be psychologically ready to buy more courses, which could be of higher value.

Hence, sales funnel is a basket of products, services or courses which range in price from nothing to a few lakh and you offer free or economical products to customers initially, before moving on to costlier and more enriching products. If you offer a product worth Rs 2 lakh to a customer who does not even know you well, you are committing a mistake as the customer will not be psychologically ready to invest so much in the first go. But if you offer a free or economical product worth a few thousands, the customer may not mind buying it. Once he tests your credibility after consuming or experiencing the first product, because of higher confidence, now you can offer them other products.

I committed a mistake during 2012 to 2017 when I used to call people to a seminar and pitch products and courses worth Rs 2-3 lakh, and of course, many customers were not ready to buy it.

Then I launched 'The Magic of Thinking Rich' (TMTR) programme, under which I give free sessions for twenty-eight days. I spent a lot of money in marketing the programme in advance, thereby creating a good interest level. Thousands of people who attended the programme, know me better now as they have seen me delivering an inspiring and value adding session every day for a month and then later on, they were ready to buy various higher value courses, which cater to the needs of their family members.

It could be a business coaching course for them or a commando training programme (held in morning hours) for their wife and children. Now you can imagine a funnel which has TMTR at the top and other programmes like YouTube mastery, Book writing coaching, Business coaching, Commando training, Sales Brahmastra and Breakthrough personality, etc., as we move lower down the funnel which becomes narrower towards the bottom. Pricewise, we have cheaper courses at the top and costliest courses at the bottom. In between, we have many courses in the mid-price range.

I have explained this transparently so that you understand how a sales funnel works and can make you a millionaire just like it did for me. My goal is to help people, but without a sales funnel, there is no way I could have done so.

Now, I would like you to take a white sheet of paper or a chart paper and draw a funnel which becomes narrower towards the bottom. Now, write your products or courses from top to bottom of the funnel. You may also keep more than one programmes/courses along the same horizontal bar, which may have a similar price range.

The longer the funnel from top to bottom, the better will be the sales.

Importance of Powerful Opening in Sales

Any good sales professional must keep in mind and follow the following eight steps while beginning any sales call or discussion. These calls could be in the form of a webinar or physical one to one session. Let's have a look at these steps:

1. **Introduction**: Begin the session with high energy level and on a positive note. Talk about where you come from and what you stand for. Explain how you have previously assisted people in building their business or career and how you can work with the customer to achieve the same goals.

2. **Appreciation**: Always begin with appreciation of the customer. You can appreciate them for their time which they have given you. They could have done many other things during the next 30-60 minutes, but they chose to speak with you. That is reason enough for you to appreciate them.
3. **Set agenda and expectations**: It's always important to set the agenda and fix the time. You can say that you would be speaking with the client for the next thirty minutes and request them to pay full attention as this call could be the best investment of the time for the customer. Tell them that at the end of the meeting, they would have full clarity on what you can do for their business and how can you help them grow their business many times over.

Set realistic goals, and after you've set them, stick to them with honesty and integrity. If you have said that the meeting will take thirty minutes, finish all that you wanted to discuss within the stipulated timeframe. It always gives a good impression, and as you know, the first impression is the last impression.

1. **Share how this agenda is going to help them**: Always remember – everyone wants to hear what is going to benefit him/her. Say clearly how this session is going to benefit him/her and what kind of benefits the person is going to get. This is a stage of indirect selling through the art of storytelling. For example, you can say - "Mr ABC purchased this product and he found more than 20% raise in the productivity of his company. Then he advised ten of his friends to buy this product." Or else, you can say – "This product will help you build high energy level among your employees, and as a result, your people retention problems will narrow down to a minimum. People bring profits. With your

people problems getting sorted out, you can easily see an increase in your profitability by 25%. This is the minimum guarantee and actually companies have seen much bigger increase in their outcomes. You can also speak with Mr XYZ or Mr LMN who had purchased this product earlier and have realized more than 35% increase in their profitability."

2. **Request no interruption**: You can switch off your phone; or put it on silent and keep it upside down. You can also request the customer to do the same. This will facilitate uninterrupted conversation which is vital for a focused and fruitful discussion.

3. **Request to invite other decision makers**: You do not want to hear from the potential customer at the end of your talk that he is not the decision maker and would like to discuss with his partner or wife. All of your efforts could be for naught if the sale does not go through. The person to whom you have discussed the situation may never be able to communicate it to the other decision makers. It's your product and you should be talking about it to decision makers. Hence, invite all decision makers before you begin the call. It is better to ask him if he is the sole decision maker and if he is not, please be candid in asking to call other decision makers as well.

4. **Take permission for asking questions**: Selling is the process of probing and invoking questions so that you can clarify some of the doubts which the customer may have, but may not be willing to ask. Hence, please take permission before asking some of the questions which may be offensive to the customer. Remember, you are dealing with people and being courteous is an important aspect of selling. You can say something like – "Sir, can I ask you

few personal questions? This will help me in letting you know the product better. Hope it's fine. However, please feel free to not answer a question if you do not feel like..." Then you can ask questions related to his family and number of children in case you are selling a family insurance coverage plan. These are the finer skills which you must master as a sales person.

5. **Acknowledge**: Always acknowledge the time and attention which the person has given to you. Be respectful for his time and attention, which actually is a gift, as even if the person does not buy the product in that call – to take an extreme example – he may still remember you and your offerings and may either recommend these products to other friends or himself buy the product later on.
6. **Keep call control with you**: Always remember to keep the control of the call in your hand. Most sales people lose the sale as they are not able to keep the control of the call and customer takes away the call control by speaking something which is out of the context or behaving in a different way. You must build solid skill set so that the customer is completely engaged during this sales call with you. This comes with experience and also with learning with the right mentors in the right environment.

Let us take a live demonstration. Here is how I could make the opening of a selling process, though this is just an example and there could be variations in this. Let's now go through a complete example of making an opening.

> *Hi Mr ABC, my name is Bhupenddra Singh Raathore. I have come from Think Rich India Pvt Ltd and our company has only one motto and that is to ensure that every person who works with*

us begins to earn ten times more than what he is earning. Not only that, that he or she also lives a stress free, fulfilling and joyful life. They should live life fully in all aspects. Thank you so much sir for giving me this opportunity as every minute of your time which you give me, you give a part of your life. As people say – time is money, I say – time is everything. Hence, I truly appreciate your time. Thanks again. By the way, I loved your office; it is so creatively designed and that makes me excited to be in a place where people value creativity and innovation. This is one of the core values for us and I am happy to be here.

Sir, I would be asking a few questions which I hope you would not mind answering. This is to help you understand the offering better.

I am sure this discussion would be highly beneficial for you as we have many joyful clients; many of whom are well known industrialists in the city and you might know them.

Sir, my first question would be – do you have any partner in the business? If you have some partners, it would be better if we also call them into this meeting. It may take a few minutes, but it will make this meeting much more useful for all of us.

I would be asking a few more questions, some of which might be slightly personal and hope you won't mind replying to them. In case you do not feel comfortable, please feel free to take the liberty of not replying to the questions. Sir, by the way, what is the turnover of your business? 3 crore? That is a commendable achievement sir. I don't know how many people in India who can build a company from scratch to a turnover of Rs 3 crore.

Congratulations sir. I am privileged to be talking to you as I am sure, through some planned actions, I can help you in building your business further and increasing the revenue to more than 10 crore in a few years and then it could be built more....

So now you see how a grand opening can help you build a connection with the customer, as you keep asking questions and getting replies. This is how you can take control of the discussion and progress with the process of selling. As you keep practicing, you will become better and better at this skill.

If the opening is powerful, you appear professional and trustworthy. You can follow these techniques in all sales calls – be it a physical meeting or a virtual call.

Cool, I really appreciate that you have completed five chapters of this book by now and you know a lot more about sales than before. Even if you knew all these things earlier, then here is a question for you – did you follow all of them religiously? If not, start following and you will see magical results in just a few days.

Most people think that these are too many things to keep in mind. Yes, initially when you start, these might be too many things, but once you get better and sharper, they are all very easy to follow. You will develop a system of working which will result in more sales, month on month.

Now is the time to get aggressive in our learning process, so let's begin the sixth chapter and learn more.

Chapter 6
Sales as an Art – Soft skills you should master

A great sales professional works hard to develop soft skills as sales is all about being around people.

In this chapter, we will speak more about different types of soft skills and the ways to develop them.

Communicate with Confidence

In Sales, it's important to transfer your emotions of certainty to the minds of your potential customers. You should speak with your customers with such excitement and conviction that they should imbibe your conviction. Customers are looking for safety of their investment. They want confidence about the return. If you're reading a book, customers should feel confident in the book's benefits, such as how the book has changed your life. The clients will then believe in the book's benefits. Customers look for *josh* in your words and mind as you speak about a product. People often ask me as why do I say my things with so much of excitement and energy. I can say the same content with ease and comfort as well. But I need to tell you one thing – when I conduct a webinar and speak comfortably in a moderate tone, the sale is only 30% of what it normally is when I speak with full enthusiasm and energy. *People experience your passion and conviction as you speak about the product.* Their sub-conscious mind should get the message. Sales always happen at the level of the sub-conscious mind.

Let's take an example – when I conduct webinars to sell my Commando training courses, I am always excited and energized while speaking about the benefits of the programme. Why should I not be confident when I have witnessed a miraculous and profound transformation in my life? I speak of the benefits not only in my life, but also in the lives of my mentees. I openly encourage prospective buyers to speak with my mentees. I show them recorded recommendations of my mentees. I tell them how this one programme will make them the commandos of life and how they will win even the toughest battles of life.

In the flow of conducting the webinars, I always tell people that it's important for the attendees to invest in their personal development. I tell them how I spent a few lakh rupees to learn sales and now earning at least a crore every month because of my selling skills. Even in the months which are not as shining, I am earning at least 20-30 lakhs, which is a great return on the investment which I made. I tell my audience that if they also want to earn an income which is multiple times more than what they are earning at the moment, they need to invest and buy my course which I am selling at the moment.

I always speak with full conviction as I strongly believe that these programmes can transform the lives of people, just like they did for me.

Hence, remember the first soft skill is communicating with confidence and conviction.

Importance of intonation in Sales

As we saw above, its crucial to transfer certainty in the minds of customers. Intonation of your voice is an important tool to transfer certainty to customers. Your tone should be different based on the situation.

Suppose your potential customer says that they do not have money at the moment. Now, you should have the tone of concern. You tell them that you agree to their thinking, but they should also realize that unless they make a change in their life and take a new decision, they will always see the same results in their life and money will always elude them. If they do not take the decision of buying now, they will be deprived of the benefits of the course and will not be able to drastically enhance their financial condition. Then while maintaining the same tone of concern, you can give them some options to invest. May be, they can invest 50% of money now and remaining can be deposited later on, after fifteen days. Theywill get the course now and will start working on the actions to make a progress in their life. Here, the tone is that of concern.

Suppose the customer says that he needs to speak with his spouse before investing. Now you can use the tone of surprise.

"Sir, what are you saying? Do you think managing your finances and enhancing your earning is your wife's responsibility or your responsibility?"

You can further explain how their spouse will never understand the earnings and rewards which he is going to get out of the programme. He can surely speak with his wife, but this will only add to his confusion and keep him in his current position, which is that of stagnation.

You can also use the tone of aggression. If someone asks you about your product and its features, you can say the benefits with excitement and energy. Customers should feel your aggressive conviction about the products. You should give your example as well as the example of your customers, who reaped huge benefits. You should say all of this in the tone of aggression. You can say – "Sir, with due respect, you might have spent ten lakh rupees in earning a management degree. But here while spending just ten thousand rupees, which is only 1% of that investment, you are thinking so much. Sir, here is a programme which, at a negligible investment, will give you multiple returns."

You can also use the tone of withdrawal. For example, you can give examples of other customers who had an appetite and hence invested in the programme. Looks like this customer does not have the same hunger, and hence he will be losing on the immense benefits. You can, in a subtle way, remind him that hunger is crucial for anyone's success, and that this customer is going to lose due to his lack of hunger. This tone may provoke an internal dialogue in the customer's mind, who may change his mind, and buy your product as he may find a genuine connection with what you have said – without hunger no one can change his/her life. That is the fact of life, after all!

You can use the tone of disappointment.

You can also use an angry tone.

Appreciate the importance of intonation in sales. Practice and master it.

Importance of Body Language in Sales

I would like to share a few important tips on how powerful your body language could be for being a good salesperson. Your body language should change as per the tone in your voice as a salesperson.

If you are aggressive in the process of selling, your body language should exude aggression. If you are considerate, your body language should show concern and consideration. If you are sad, your face should reflect sadness. If you are curious, your facial expression should show curiosity.

Your dressing habits are also important. Your dressing should be either at the same level as that of your clients or – even better still – you should be one step up. Suit, tie or coat reflect authority. As I said – sales is more about sub-conscious and less about the conscious process. Your body language and the way you dress will help a lot in building a rapport and influence on the customer.

Your body language should reflect that of your customer. You will create a stronger rapport if you reflect the body language of your customers.

Importance of Storytelling in Sales

Storytelling is an important art in sales. You can tell a story about your company or products. You can tell the story of your journey. You need to choose a specific story depending on the psychology of the customer. You need to have at least thirty stories about your company or products. For example, in my webinars on 'Breakthrough Personality', I told my story to the audience. I told them how weak I was in my English communication. I lacked confidence and was poor at interpersonal communication. Then I tell them how, by working on my personality, I became wealthy and successful. Customers relate to this story and buy my products. I have made a sale of Rs 8-9 lakhs in one webinar as well through the powerful use of storytelling.

Somewhere, I tell the story of my own failure or the story of someone else's failure. Sometimes I tell people my story of how I bought a course despite all my family members stopping me from investing in the course on personality development. They did not know whether there would be any benefit from this programme. I tell the audience how I was afraid of taking the decision because no one supported me. I was alone, and I knew the stakes were high. But then I took the decision to go ahead with the investment and see the benefit of this one decision. I was more nervous than you might be, and today, I am receiving a lakh times more benefits, if not more. I am earning crores of rupees every month, and I am sure you will also get the benefits.

When customers hear the story, they can correlate with my story and decide to go ahead in purchasing the course.

In storytelling, one very important aspect is to tell the stories of contrast. What does it mean? It means you tell customers the story of one of your clients who had a turnover of Rs 90 lakhs and has now improved his business turnover to Rs 24 crores. You see the contrast. People need to hear the stories of contrast or else they will not be clearly convinced about the benefits of your products, services or courses. I tell them the story of how a famous car dealer who was into selling premium cars, attended my 'Business Mastery' programme and could sell ninety cars in the very next month as compared to only forty cars which he normally sold earlier.

Hence, contrast stories will always help you sell more.

My suggestion is – please watch all the recordings of sales webinars which I have conducted. You will get a lot of insights from these. These are actual sales webinars many of which are available as a part of my e-Learning courses. In case of doubt, please contact my team.

Importance of Rapport building in Sales

Suppose you are in a foreign land and you see a person wearing familiar clothes. You ask the person – "Hey are you from India?" And he smiles back and responds in affirmation. Automatically, you initiate the conversation with the person and if the person is also from the same state as yours, the rapport becomes deeper. You both begin talking about numerous things in common, such as food, clothing, and your friends from the same state who live in that country. And if the individual is from the same city as you, you will bond like long-lost friends and exchange numbers, in addition to sharing many other pleasantries. This is how relationships are built.

You might have a few people who are really good at building rapport with others. They will speak with people about things that people care about and build a strong bond in no time.

By keeping the same or similar body language, you can build a rapport too.

There are four ways of rapport building, using the body language.

Matching: If you are sitting with a person across the table, keep your right hand in the same pose as his. If the other person is moving his left hand in a certain way, you also move your left hand. It has to be done subtly. It gives a feeling of comfort and familiarity to the other person and helps build a good rapport. With gradual awareness and practice, it will become a part of you and your sales call or meeting. Matching can have a built-in 'time lag'. For example, if a seated client uncrosses his legs and leans slightly inward while speaking, you should wait for a few seconds and then discretely adopt the same posture.

Mirroring: Mirroring refers to the simultaneous 'copying' of the behaviour of another person, as if reflecting their movements back to them. When done with respect and discretion, mirroring creates a positive feeling of responsiveness in you and others. Here, if your customer extends his left hand towards the front, you can extend your right hand. Due to the mirroring effect, your right hand and the customer's left hand look in the same line. Often, this looks more relatable to the customer, as you both are sitting as a mirror image of each other and your right hand is actually aligned with his left hand.

Leading: As you practice matching and mirroring with your audience or the client, you gradually start leading and influencing the behaviour and body language of others. What it means is – if you change the movement of your right hand, people may also change – in a sub-conscious way – the position of their right hand in order to match the position of your hand. This means – the audience has developed a rapport with you. This cause and effect movement is applicable to both matching and mirroring.

I give a live demonstration of this in my seminars. After talking about these concepts in a two-day-long seminar, I ask people to freeze, and then I walk amidst the audience and show them clearly how all 4-5 people sitting on one table are actually keeping both legs in a similar position. I also show them how people who have been sitting at the same table in another corner, in a sub-conscious way, have been keeping their right hand, for example in the same position. This feels almost magical to people.

Pacing: This means matching the pace of the client. For example, if the client is speaking at a certain pace, you can also learn to speak at a similar pace. If the client is batting his eyelids at the pace of twenty-five blinks in a minute, I am also matching this pace. If the other person is breathing in at a rate of fifteen breaths per minute, you can follow this pace. This can also be done in terms of words. For example, if the other person is using the word 'financial' again and again, you can make your offer while talking about how his financial issues will be sorted out after attending the course. If the other person is talking about America again and again, you can – while giving your examples – can use America as the country. You can also match the tone. If the other person is speaking in a reflective tone, you can also speak in a reflective tone.

There are five more ways to build rapport which are mentioned below:

Appreciation: One of the best ways to build a rapport is to appreciate someone. When you appreciate someone, they feel the secretion of dopamine, which makes them happy.

Permission: You also build better rapport by seeking permission before asking a question. This makes others feel in a position of power and control, and helps build better rapport.

Acknowledgement: You also acknowledge the points made by others to build a better rapport.

Verbal nodes: You can say words like – Okay... hmmm ... right... noted, etc. These are verbal nodes which help you with a better rapport.

Paraphrasing: Paraphrasing means to state something written or spoken in different words, especially in a shorter and simpler form to make the meaning clearer. This is a crucial part of any dialogue or negotiation meeting. You can summarize the points made by others in your own words. For example, "Okay, I see the point you are making. We need to have a better system for having two-way communication and keeping you updated on a weekly basis. Absolutely right. I will surely put up a mechanism for a weekly review. It's a great idea. In fact, I was about to make this suggestion. Thanks for making this point."

Another example could be, "Thank you sir. I see that you want more work on content and greater depth so that the customers connect better with the advertisement. We will do that and will come back to present again, in a week's time. Hope this is fine."

Paraphrasing, as you can make out by now, does help in rapport building and creating a better and more satisfying experience for the customer.

Dealing with status quo barrier in Sales

Many times, customers do not buy because they worry about changing the status. A good salesperson challenges the same mindset of maintaining the status quo. Many people think of family and society, which may make them question why someone is buying this new product? For example, someone is happy with his existing car and is not sure why he should buy a new, bigger, and costlier one! You should tell such customers that as you buy a new and bigger car, your prestige in society will go up. Through the law of attraction, you will start being surrounded by more successful people. Your thinking will shift, and you will think more broadly. Because your actions are a result of your ideas, you will notice a significant change in your life. Can you guess how this all began? By buying a new and bigger car? This is how one decision can change your life in a magical but sure shot way.

It's important to break the status quo barrier of your customer. People are lazy by nature and do not want to take any action to change their current way of living, thinking or acting. Its important at times for a salesperson to 'break' that pre cast and long-lasting mould of thinking. It's important to challenge your customers. Use calculations to demonstrate the benefits to customers. For challenging the status quo, many times, you need to create the need. Often, people do not know whether they 'need' it. Need is there, but it's hidden within them. Or else, the need is not immediate. You can create the need with following statements:

"You should have worked on your personality ten years ago. But for some reason, if you could not do it, now is the time for you to improve your personality. I have a course for personality transformation and you should go for it now. It's one life and you are already late. Don't you think so?"

You can take the example of iPhone. Apple will keep on creating the need by adding new and more useful features in its iPhones. Or else, why on this earth people who already have an iPhone feel the need to buy a new one?

Importance of Public Speaking in Sales

You need to believe in the fact that this one skill of public speaking can make you the Prime Minister of India. Public Speaking is the best resource for being a good salesperson. If you do not become a good salesperson, you will keep reaching people individually. That is going to take a lot of time. Public speaking will let you reach out to thousands of people and thereby you can reach out to millions of people at a fast pace. You can address many people at the same time.

Hence, learn the art of Public speaking and practice it every day. Join programmes and read books on mastering the art of public speaking. Be in the company of people who are better speakers than you. Learn what they are doing differently to become such great speakers. Learn, practice and improve as a public speaker and the day is not far when you will use this skill to expand your horizons as a salesperson.

NO - Next Opportunity

Picture a situation when you are selling your product or service to someone and get rejected. You try selling to one customer, and it does not work out. You try selling to another customer, and that also does not work out. You get demotivated and lose heart.

But you should always remember one thing – if you get a 'No', you should move on to the next opportunity.

Don't sell for the sake of commission. Do it for a 'mission'. Make sales a part of your mission and leave the thought of making 'sales only for commission' to others. Thinkbig, as sales is one of the biggest professions in the world, and this is one path that can give you all that you always wanted in life.

So, whenever you hear a NO, you should hear – Next Opportunity. You just need to move on to the next person.

Common mistakes to be avoided in Sales

In this book, we will talk about three mistakes which many salespersons do and lose the order. I do not want you to make the same mistakes and hence let's straightway move to those three mistakes.

Mistake no 1: To give too less or too much information.

Frequently, you do not adequately explain the product and do not provide information on all of its characteristics. The buyer may be looking for a certain feature about which you did not provide any information. Maybe he was looking for product durability, and you did not touch upon this benefit at all. Hence, the customer assumed that the product was not durable and did not go ahead with the purchase decision. Or maybe, the customer assumed that there was no service backup as you gave lots of information on the product features, but said nothing about the service support.

On the contrary, salespeople also give too much information. For example, if you are selling a washing machine, you may go overboard while talking about the internal circuitry, or colour or the country of manufacturing, which the customers are not interested in. Rather, they might be looking for economy and quality of washing, service support, etc. Hence, you gave too much information, which did not help the customer.

I have seen many cases where people from a network marketing background will talk a lot about the international background of the products ("This is being manufactured in Malaysia and Vietnam; it is a hit there. Now only it has come to India.") in order to impress the customer. What they should actually do is to talk about how the features of the product will help the customer earn more money in his business. Superficial knowledge will not help the customer.

I have seen people give too many testimonials to customers. It's not required. You should have 2-3 good testimonials and ask the customer to visit a website or link where they can see more testimonials. Or else, you can tell the customers that you need to ask more previous customers whether they would be interested in giving a testimonial. Customers will appreciate this.

The second mistake that the salespeople commit is they describe the features of the products as per their own preference or liking. They should instead describe the features as per the customer's preference. For example, if you are selling a washing machine to a person who operates it, you have to speak of the features related to ease and quality of washing. While selling the same washing machine to the person who has to make the purchase, you need to speak about safety, cost, service, EMI options, etc. Each customer has his or her own unique way of looking at the same product.

This is known as "sales positioning". If you are selling an iPhone to a businessman, you have to speak about the features that will help him do his business better. For example, how the businessman can share his documents and presentations with his customers, etc. If you're selling the same iPhone to a student, mention the high-resolution selfie camera, photo sharing features, and video editing features if he's also a content creator. Every customer is looking for a few key features and a good salesperson knows which features to pitch in to which customer.

The third mistake that salespersons make is that they are not able to give a point to the customer which makes them a unique seller, product or service provider. When a customer goes to a supplier and asks , "Why should I buy from you?" the regular response is:

"We have the best features and service."

"We have the lowest cost."

Now, which seller will not say this? This response will not set you in a unique place.

Your response has to be unique and different.

For example, if a customer comes to me, I say the following:

"We have a strong belief that we will give 1000 times the return on investment to the customers. We are living to impact fifty million lives. We have a unique philosophy: when you support people selflessly, the world supports you endlessly. We have so far positively impacted the lives of thirty-five lakh people and will positively impact the lives of fifty crore people by 12 January 2030. One of our unique programmes, 'The Magic of Thinking Rich' is a free programme for twenty-eight days. This programme will be free for forty-five days, out of which the programme will be in Hindi for twenty-one days. We are the only company to conduct a programme on such a massive scale that thousands of people join at the same time. I am the only trainer from India to have gone to deliver a talk in United Nations Organizations...."

Hence, the customer should get a unique impression about your product and the company.

One of the salespersons who came to me recently said that he was from a company which has invented a breakthrough toothpaste. Look at my conversation with him.

"How long have you been in the market?"

"Sir, we are here for more than ten years in India and twenty years in the world."

"Is it not surprising that I have not heard of your product despite being in the Indian market since the last decade?"

"Sir, it's because our product is sold through word of mouth?"

"But then even Amway products are sold through word of mouth. I have heard about that product, but am yet to hear about your company or product. I have also heard of Patanjali product..."

He did not have any satisfactory reply to my questions.

Then I asked, "How is your product unique and different?"

"Sir, our product has a mix of seven herbs..."

"How many herbs does Patanjali toothpaste have?"

"Sir, that I do not know..."

Now you tell me, how do I get a feeling that the toothpaste that he is trying to sell is unique? One has to do a proper research and study to find the uniqueness of one's products before pitching it to the customer.

Remember the three mistakes which salespersons commonly make and you should avoid.

1. To say too much or too less
2. Not talking of the product as per customers' needs
3. Not bringing out the uniqueness of products

Don't commit these mistakes. You are with me and I want you to be the best salesperson.

Situation Based Selling

Now the question is, how to sell in a corporate setting where there are multiple decision-makers involved in the process of buying? Are you still going to use the usual sales techniques? The answer is that in the case of corporations, you need to frame your statements or questions based on the situation. Here, the customers are highly qualified, and often carry a big ego.

Your soft skills matter even more here.

Here, you will find junior, middle, and senior management people involved in the buying process. In such set-up, you need to dress perfectly in a suit, trousers, tie, shoes, and belt where you need to match the colours professionally.

Here, you need to do situation-based selling. You can ask them why they bought the product. They will most likely tell you about the situation and problems.

Suppose they ask you questions about the higher price; you can say the following.

"Sir, your company could have kept people with lower salary instead of you. But it has hired you as you can deliver a value which a less professional person can never provide. Our price is slightly higher, but believe me sir, you will realize that our quality is far superior than others." You have to show them evidences.

You can also say, "Sir, I know you have got a lower quotation from another trainer, but the values which our trainer will provide are beyond any comparison. You can yourself check sir, how many training programmes the other trainer has conducted? How many lives have they transformed? On the other hand, we have conducted many programmes and you can talk to any of our clients. Our value is proven and hence we are charging slightly higher, but its insignificant in comparison to the value and lifelong transformation which our trainers are going to offer. Let's take an example of KBC. Can you get someone other than Amitabh Bachchan for conducting the show? I am sure we can't even imagine. Sir, in a training programme, everything depends on the quality and uniqueness of the trainer, and hence a comparison only on the fee will not really make real sense. Hence, we will request you to consider our offer keeping in mind the value which we offer. You will be thrilled from the experience."

Situation based selling while conversing with the corporate clients is the key here.

Role of Motivation in Sales

It has become fashionable for people to say that motivation does not do anything. They couldn't be more wrong. Motivation can do what no other initiative can do, and it is surely a daily need for a salesperson. Those who have seen the movie '*Founder*' which is the story of a salesperson who creates the brand name known as McDonald's worldwide today, know the power of daily motivation. He listens to the motivational audio tapes every day in the evening when he comes back to the hotel after facing numerous rejections.

Declare the date of your expiry!

What does it mean? It means that you declare the date when your older version will die and your new version will be born. My birthday falls on 12 January. This year, I have declared that Bhupenddra Singh Raathore's 90 kg weight will expire and a new, leaner and fitter BSR will be born. Declare such dates, a few examples of which are as follows:

On the date… …., the old version (your name) who was shy of selling will die and a new version (your name) will be born – one who loves selling and enjoys earning money.

On the date… …., the old version (your name) who thought earning money is difficult, will die and a new version (your name) who knows that earning money is super easy will be born.

On the date… …., when the old version (your name) who does not set daily sales goals will die and the new version (your name) who sets and achieves daily goals, will be born.

Declare the date of expiry of your older version. This is a great way to send the right signal to your sub-conscious brain.

To cite my example, I still motivate myself every day in the morning. This motivation is required because a salesperson has daily goals and actions that fall into the following four categories. In the case of rejection, you need to motivate. You need to work for a minimum of 12-14 hours. Then you have to spend two hours for your health and enrichment. You can catch up with sleep for 6-8 hours.

Let's look at the following four categories of actions you must indulge in every day:

1. How many new prospects you spoke with?
2. How many old prospects you followed up with?
3. How many demonstrations you gave?
4. How many closures you had, meaning in how many cases you got money?

My way of generating prospects is through Facebook ads. You need to decide how to generate prospects. It could be through talks, references, cold calling, etc.

Repeat this sentence many times today, "In sales, those who do not bring results, bring excuses." And excuses could be of many types. You can blame slower market growth, poor products, poor after sales service, or foolishness of customers. Or else, you can get orders, come what may. You decide whether you want to get orders or make excuses.

You should repeat every day, "Difficulty is in the minds of people."

If you do not bring results, you will not only make your lives miserable, you will also make the life of your family and society miserable.

If you ask me, you just need one quality for selling – you need to have the *junoon*.

If a person does not eat betel leaf or *gutkha,* he feels uncomfortable.

If a person who loves rice doesn't eat rice for a day, he feels uncomfortable.

If a person loves smoking, he will feel uncomfortable if he does not smoke for a day.

Similarly, if I do not sell even for a day, I do not feel comfortable.

If I do not get money , I feel terrible. I feel something is missing.

If I do not follow up with old prospects, I think I am missing something.

All the four actions are my daily goal, and hence, even if I miss out on any one of these, I feel uncomfortable. I feel something is missing and it makes me unnerved.

A salesperson has got to be smart. For example, you can ask for a cup of tea if you go to meet someone. In our culture, a cup of tea is a well-accepted norm and you can use the time, and you will get a minimum of 8-10 minutes before the tea is served, to break ice with the customer. You can ask for his permission to share a few queries and engage him in a conversation which will bring you sales. A salesperson is always a smart person and hence no surprises that 90% of CEOs are from sales background. They are all great salespersons.

Master the soft skills mentioned in this chapter. This is going to take time and effort, but the efforts would fetch you crores for sure.

Chapter 7
Importance of asking the right questions in Sales

Every salesperson has a powerful weapon, and that is the freedom to ask relevant questions. If a salesperson masters the art of asking the right questions, they can win big in sales. When you go for a sales meeting, ensure that the customer speaks more and you speak less. The customer should speak 70% of the time. Your task is to probe and ask questions.

This chapter is dedicated to the art of asking relevant questions.

Let's begin with an example of what a question should look like.

"Sir, you would have bought the product had it been 20% cheaper. This means you like the product. It is just a matter of a discount of Rs 5,000 after which you will buy the product. You have already agreed to pay Rs 20,000. With an additional investment of 20%, the product or course will be yours. Would you help me understand why you are unsure about the product beyond Rs 20,000?"

Make a customer speak at regular intervals. This is possible through the process of questioning. Each word that your customer says will give you clues to explain a certain feature of the product or adjust your pricing a bit to sell the product. If you continue to speak about your product without allowing the consumer to speak, you will not know what is keeping him stuck and preventing the sale from happening. You will not know the true and previously unknown reason why the buyer has not purchased the product thus far. Sales do not happen when it is merely to earn a commission. Sales happen when it is for a mission. A salesperson values his customers not only for paying a few thousand rupees, but also for the fact that a happy customer can share a good word in his own community, which may comprise thousands of people. Hence, focus on keeping customers delighted with your products and services, and you will see your business grow. Keep this fact in mind.

Look at your customers carefully. Some of the customers may not have bought a course worth a large sum, but their network might be huge, and they may bring in a large number of customers by referring your name. Hence, worship your customers and give them immense value. This is at the core of selling.

Before adding value to a customer, ask for permission. For example, you can send a message to customers before adding them to your broadcast list which, could be as follows: "Sir, I share some useful and actionable links with my esteemed stakeholders every other day. I have been in this field for many years, and I have come across many useful pieces of information that people can follow to make their lives better. Can I add you to my broadcast link?" And once you add them, keep your word. Every alternate day, the message must go. At the same time, it should not happen every day.

Questioning is an important technique to understand someone's mindset, but you need to get permission even before asking a question.

For example, you can ask, "Sir, can I ask you why you are unsure of buying this product?". Suppose the customer says that he had earlier bought the product and had a bitter experience. You can say, "Sir, can I say something here?" Then you can say. "Sir, I am sorry that you had a bitter experience, but do you feel one wrong experience will lead to more such bad experiences? If you took an Uber ride and had an unprofessional experience, does that mean that you will stop using Uber? Do you think other Uber drivers will not be better and more professional? If you go to a gym and do not like the machines, does that mean you will stop exercising? Will you not try another gym or adopt other means of exercising?"

It is important here that you ask questions only after seeking permission. The customer's need for recognition and 'being in the driving seat of making the buying decision' must always be respected and protected, or else you will miss the sale.

Paraphrasing is another tool you must use to sell more. So, what does paraphrase mean?

Let me cite an example. Suppose the customer says, "Earlier, I had met a salesperson from your company. He promised me big benefits but never turned up on time for forthcoming meetings. He did not clarify my queries and did not bother with anything other than getting money. He did not even listen to me. He was the most undisciplined salesperson I have ever met."

You can say, "Sir, thank you for sharing your thoughts. Can I make some comments?"

After taking permission, you can add, "Sir, I understand your concern. You met an unprofessional salesperson who could not evoke any trust in you. He was not punctual or sincere. I would like to use this opportunity to change your perception of our company. I will explain the benefits of the product now and be ready in time for all such forthcoming discussions. You can decide not to place any order if you find me late for any meeting. I want you to experience timeliness, punctuality, and listenability in our salespersons and I would like you to experience this through me. Thank you for sharing your unpleasant past experience, or else I would not have had this opportunity to clarify and correct this perception. Making and keeping 100% of customer delighted is our goal and you will experience this. By the way, I have summarized your past experience as told to me, I hope you know that you are speaking with a salesperson who listens deeply."

In the above example, you have seen the application of seeking permission, paraphrasing as well as giving assurance. Now, as you keep your words through actions, you will regain the trust of the customer and the sales will follow.

Objection handling is related to the art of questioning and answering questions. Let's have a look at this.

Objection handling:

Roshni (name changed), one of my past customers from Indore who had purchased a business coaching programme worth Rs 50,000 a few years ago, came to attend a recent programme in which I was selling the business coaching programme for Rs 3,50,000. Now, the programmes are going to be conducted in metros, including Delhi and Mumbai. None of the programmes will be conducted in Indore this time.

At the end of the programme, Roshni came to me, "Sir, I wanted to join this programme as the last programme that I attended was many years ago. You also spoke about many new benefits, but sir, now the cost has gone up to seven times the old cost and I will have to travel outside Indore."

I instantly said, "You decide Roshni. If you delay taking the programme at the current investment of Rs 3,50,000, after a few years, you will take the same programme for Rs 10 lakh or more. Don't miss the training. Also, earlier I had clients only from Indore. Now bigger businessmen from metros are joining my programmes, and hence the programme is held among a much larger and prestigious clientele. As the cost has risen seven times by now, it will keep rising in future as the value is rising even faster. You decide, you want to miss the bus or catch it!."

You see the confidence. If you are confident about your product, others can see through it and will be more interested in buying from you.

In sales, be prompt and ready with your answers and solutions. Your conviction will go a long way in selling your products and courses.

Sales and Agreement Frame Questions (AFQ)

Psychologists say that any person who initially agrees with you a few times is highly likely to agree with you when you tell him the price and other details of your programme. Hence, your initial questioning technique plays an important role in getting your sales done.

Also, if a customer initially agrees with you, he will find it difficult to disagree later on, as by disagreeing with you subsequently, he will be contradicting himself.

Let me cite two examples here. The first is an example of a child, and the second is an example of a customer.

You – "Hi Bittu, between both your parents, who do you love more; Papa or Mummy?

Bittu – "I love both..."

You – "Great! Mummy cooks food for you and takes care of all your needs before you go to the school. Does she, or doesn't she?"

Bittu – "Yes, she does..."

You – "Does Papa take you to the malls and restaurants? Does he get you the toys...yes or no?"

Bittu – "Yes..."

You – "Now, would you mind studying an hour every day in the evening to make your parents happy? Yes or no?"

Bittu – "Yes..."

Now you see here, after saying yes to some of the initial questions, Bittu finds it easy to say yes for his studies, too.

The advantage of an agreement frame question is to let people know that the decision is being taken by them. Nobody wants others to force them into making buying decisions. People want to make their buying decisions themselves. Through AFQ, you give this power to the customers, and your sale happens in a mutually win-win environment. You also help the customer make the right decision.

Also, hope you have noted that you should give two options at the end of each question to make it easy for the person to respond.

You can use AFQ technique in your office, work as well as in family life. Let's take the second example with another customer.

You – "Do you really want to become great? Yes or no?"

Customer – "Yes!"

You – "And in order to become great, you have to build some skills? Do you agree or not?"

Customer – "Yes."

You – "And among all the skills, selling skills is very important. Yes or no?"

Customer – "Yes."

You – "People who know this skill, are living a better life. Selling skill is important in all areas, be it the field of politics, business, corporates, etc. You think and tell me whether its right or wrong?"

Customer – "Right."

You – "So when should you learn this skill, today or tomorrow… ?"

Customer – "Today…"

You – "And do you feel we are late even if we learn this skill today, as actually you should have learnt this skill ten years ago?"

Customer – "Yes."

You – "Do you think you are going to use this skill for lifetime? You will get benefits from this one skill forever and will keep earning more and more?"

Customer – "Yes."

You – "Do you think the price which you are going to pay is nothing in comparison with the prosperity which this skill is going to bring to your life...?

Customer – "Yes..."

Now you see the power of AFQ. In fact, using this, you can convince people to say things that you want them to say. For example, if you want people to say 'Diwali', you can simply ask, "There is one festival that was celebrated on the occasion of Lord Rama coming back to his kingdom after defeating the demon king Ravana. Do you know which festival it is?"

If you are a sales manager with a team that does not believe in the above sentence, you need to coach the team members using agreement frame questions to start believing in this sentence. Some of the questions which you may ask are as follows:

"You live just once. Right or wrong?"

"Don't you think you need to be super rich to fulfil all your dreams in this one life? Yes or no?"

"Don't you think you need to learn the art of sales to be super rich? Yes or no?"

"Don't you think you can learn this skill just like many do? Yes or no?"

Agreement Frame Questions:

"Sir, do you want to grow your business?"

"Do you think learning a new skill to improve your inter-personal skills will be good for you?"

You need to use all these questions to close the sale.

Another word of caution for you - never make any direct statement while guessing about the customer. Instead, guide the customer to think and decide for themselves.

For example, if you get the feeling that a potential customer is having financial problems and hence is not able to take the decision, you should never ask – "Sir, I think you are facing financial problems. Is this correct?" The other person will never agree.

Instead, you can say, "Sir, as we know 90% of people in the country are facing financial problems. Do you agree with this?" Most likely, he will answer in agreement. And then he may open up about his problem. Even if he does not, never be the first to make a personal statement about someone. Nobody wants to admit that he is having financial problems himself or herself. But everyone will be happy to admit that a majority of people are going through financial troubles.

The goal behind these questions is to make the customer realize his true problems and think of possible solutions while thinking about your product as one of the key solutions.

Now you know the power of AFQ. Use it in your personal and professional life and practice it every day. Make it fun and soon you will be a great salesperson, thereby becoming prosperous, joyful and successful.

AFQ is also very useful if you want to win a debate while still making both the parties feel good.

Start practicing it from today and make it a habit. Remember – 'practice makes us perfect'.

Direct Questions

Often, you see that the customer is in a closed zone and is not opening to sales. He is under doubt. In such a case, you ask a direct question and bring him out of the zone of indecision and inaction. For example, you can say, "Sir, I know that you do not want to purchase the product as you are in doubt. I also know that you are currently struggling in your life and are sad. Am I right or wrong?"

Now, this is a direct question and can shock the customer a bit. This shock is needed to change the pattern of his thinking.

I have said this in a few past interactions – "Sir, I know that you do not want to purchase the product, and this act of indecisiveness has kept you struggling for many years. I know that you may keep struggling for many years and will not come out of this challenging situation easily. Please pardon me, but am I right or wrong?"

This kind of questioning is to be done rarely and as a last resort to break the self-created mould in which the customer has cocooned himself. This cocoon needs to be broken not only for you to sell, but primarily for the customer to buy and change his life for good reasons. Or else, the customer will once again miss the chance to bring more shine into his life. If you truly believe in your product, you can ask such a question. If you care for the customer, he will sense your empathy and genuine concern, even in your direct and candid questioning.

Few more types of questions

Let's learn a few more types of questions. You might have heard of an open-ended question. Examples could be:

"Sir, I know that you want to buy the product. You might have a few reasons. I would be happy to know some of the reasons why you want to buy the product."

"Sir, let's keep sales aside for some time. I would be happy to know about your experiences running your business in the last ten years or so. How has business been? Have you faced some challenges, and you may also share something about your wins and success stories?"

These are **open-ended questions** as these make the customers speak. And as the customer shares some of his experiences, you can pick some pointers based on his sayings and pitch in sales again. Many times, you will get vital input about why the customer is not able to buy and the questions which are crossing his mind. Then, as you get more clarity about the thinking pattern of the customer, you can once again pitch in sales and close the sale.

Then comes the turn of **close-ended questions**. Here the questions could be in one sentence or in limited words. For example, in agreement frame questions, all queries are close-ended in nature.

"Do you travel outside?"

"Do you want to grow your business?"

"Do you like adventure?"

"Do you want to increase your earning?"

The answer to all these questions would be short and mostly in a yes or no.

Next in the series on questioning technique is **directional questions**. Some of the questions could be as follows:

"Why are you earning money?"

"To enjoy a good life?"

"Have you been to any foreign country?"

"Would you like me to share with you how by spending Rs 90,000, you can visit your dream destinations like... while staying in 4-star properties? Your family would be so happy, as travelling is one of the best ways to be happy and see a new world around you. You do not have to worry at all about making any arrangements. Your pick up from your home to travelling to many countries and all the arrangements in between until you are happily back home are ours. Just like you are the expert in your work, we are the experts in ours. Hence, we are two experts talking about how to make you enjoy your life better and make it memorable. Would you like me to tell you more about the plans?"

These are directional questions.

Now, you can also ask decisional questions. Such questions are meant to help your client to make a decision. Examples of such questions are as follows:

"Sir, I would like to know why you don't want to buy this product (or service, or course)? You tell me the benefits of not buying the product. Or else, what are the losses from buying the products? I will tell you the benefits of buying. I will also tell you the disadvantage of not buying the product."

"Sir, why don't you imagine the benefits that you will get. Let's see these benefits that you will get. After thinking through the benefits, you can make your decision."

The questions mentioned above are **decision questions**.

Next in the series are **validation questions** which are asked to validate your assumption to pitch in a particular product in a particular price range or pitch in a certain type of product before the customer. Examples could be as follows:

"Sir, how many years have you been working in the company?

"10 years..."

"Are you working alone or do you have a partner?"

"I have a partner."

"How much are you and your partner earning?"

"I am earning a lakh or two in a month and my partner is earning around the same."

Based on these questions, you can validate at what price point the client will be ready to purchase the product.

Next in the series are **filtration questions**.

You ask questions that will filter through the reasons the client is unsure about purchasing the product. Then you get to the exact reason that is preventing the client from buying and you can then make your offer accordingly to help the client buy.

For example, I always ask a question – "If the price of the product was zero, would you have purchased the product?"

If the client says yes, I know he is happy with the product. It's just a matter of the price. Before asking this question, he might have given many frivolous reasons, including "I do not have time to decide on this purchase now" or "my partner would not agree", etc. But now, you know that he would like to purchase it if we just worked on the price.

You can also ask **understanding questions** with the sole intention to understand the customer and his needs better. A couple of examples are as follows:

"Sir, can you please elaborate on your key worries as a result of which you are not able to grow your business?"

"Sir, you said that your business is on a decline. Can you please suggest 2-3 reasons behind this decline in your opinion?"

Let's look at **guiding questions** which you may ask to lead the customer to where you want him to go.

"Sir, 90% of people in the country are suffering in their businesses because they are not able to communicate well with their vendors and customers. Do you think you can learn the art of public speaking so you can be better at communicating with your stakeholders?"

"Sir, you said that your company is facing a few legal issues. Do you think it's because you don't have an expert legal counsellor to guide you? Do you think having a good lawyer for the next six months could actually get you out of the problems?

Always remember – Sales is a process of realization. It's all about making the customer have a new set of realizations. Once you do that, you are close to the closure of a sales deal.

Asking the right questions

There are no restrictions on sales. India is a country of opportunity. We are a 140-crore strong country. Maybe only 1% of these people are willing to learn. Even then, it's a large number. Even if you can tap into 1% of this population, it's a population of 14 lakhs. Even if you sell a product worth Rs 100 to every customer, you are generating a revenue of Rs 14 crores!

Sales is all about looking for opportunities. As I mentioned in one of the previous chapters, when you get a 'no' from a customer, you should only hear 'next opportunity'. Keep moving to more potential customers until you see people coming to buy your products.

You need to learn certain skills to expand your sales base.

One of these skills is – asking the right questions. If you do not master this skill, you will lose many sales opportunities.

Let me cite a few examples.

A woman who attended my programme, came to me, worried. She said, "Sir, I want to attend your course, but I am a housewife. I have to take care of my husband and children, and hence I do not find time for other tasks."

As a salesperson, I had two choices. The first alternative is to get clean bowled and quit. After all, it is a valid issue. Second option , I will ask a pertinent question and enhance her hunger for buying the course. I said in this case, "Ma'am, I appreciate it, but don't you think that your personal growth and fulfilment of your life's aspirations is also your responsibility? If you do not work towards your goals, who else will work for you? And don't we all know – it's just life. Look around, and you will find many women who have made their own identity, despite being busy with the household chores. Sudha

Murthy, who is a known author and speaker, is just one example. She actually, in addition to taking care of her family, also supported her husband when he was building Infosys. Don't you think this course will make it so easy for you to become what you must become?"

Now you can see how this one question has changed her way of looking at my course.

Second example – A gentleman came to me after another programme. He said, "Sir, I am willing to join your course, but I can't afford the fee."

I asked her a question, "Tell me something about assets possessed by you. Do you have a car? Did you go on a holiday...?"

"Yes sir, I have a car…" he said.

"This course will come at a fraction of the cost of the car. It's just a matter of priority. If growth is your priority, you will find a way to achieve it. Money is rarely the reason people do not buy."

Third example – An army man came to me and said that he does not get time as he gets only a month's break every year from his Army job. I asked, "Don't you think that one month's break is good enough for you to complete my Business Brahmastra course, which is for ninety hours? You can easily spend three hours every day and complete this course in one month. If you keep learning one such course every year, in 5-6 months, you will be in a position to do what you have always been dreaming of. You can start your own company."

One right question can change the pattern of someone's thinking and break some of the barriers that they have made for themselves. Then they make the buying decision.

Questions are the most important aspect of selling.

You must have the desire to speak and ask the right questions.

You take the example of Prime Minister of India. You must have seen him asking questions on the following lines:

"Brothers and sisters, do you want to make India a world leader?"

"My dear countrymen, do you think corruption should be abolished from the country and corrupt people should be punished?"

"My dear countrymen, don't you think those who are playing with your future should not have any future in this country's politics?"

Now, majority of people in a rally are going to say yes in unison. Even if there are a few who may not agree, they do not have a choice. When TV viewers see these telecasts, they also get the same message – Prime Minister is loved by the masses. He is the future of the country. What he is saying must be right.

On a lighter note, whenever the opposition raises questions about the weaknesses of the government, the ruling party asks a question, "If not the Prime Minister, then who else?"

And even the opposition knows they do not have a clear and convincing answer.

Such is the power of questioning.

I was pursuing a contract for conducting a programme on sales for a corporation. I met the HR person and he said, "Sir, your programme is good, but it's out of our budget, as it's too costly."

I said, "Sir, you are thinking of the cost of conducting the programme. But have you ever calculated the cost of keeping untrained people in the company? Every day, your people are losing orders worth many times the cost of the training programme and this leakage is happening every single day. Your salespeople will start bagging more orders with just one training, and don't you think the monetary rewards will be several times the expense of the training programme...?"

As he was speechless, I could see that he had started thinking seriously about holding the programme now.

One leader said, "I do not need any training for me. My team should be trained."

I said, "Sir, can I ask a question?"

He nodded in affirmation.

I asked, "Sir, do you want a trained finance head or an untrained one? Do you want a trained operations head or an untrained one? Do you want a trained personal assistant or an untrained one? If the answer is yes, try asking your people if they want a trained leader or an untrained one."

I could see that he was smiling now.

It's a wrong notion that you need to convince people to sell. The right notion is, you need to ask questions to sell.

Sales FAQs

Let's practice answering some of the FAQs which you would most likely face from customers. Here, I am giving three sample questions, but you will find that all other FAQs will also fall into any of the following three categories (time, money or confusion):

FAQ 1: I want discount on the price. I am not able to pay such a high price.

Answer: Talk about the products and their benefits. Shift the focus to the pain of the customer. Don't offer a discount outright. First, talk about the customer's pain and how you can solve it. Talk about the unique features of your products. Suppose they say that they are getting the same or similar programme from a competitor at a lesser price Y, whereas your course costs X. You can correct them by saying that actually the cost of a competitor's products is X+Y, as they will first buy their products and then your products, as your products will actually serve the customer's needs. Then you can explain the unique features that only your products can offer.

FAQ 2: I do not have time…
Answer: Remind them of the losses they are making as they do the same things again and again. It's time for them to 'sharpen the saw' as suggested in a Japanese saying. It's important for them to take out some time to learn and upgrade. Only then will they get new results, which they have not gotten so far.

FAQ 3: I do not know how the product will help me. It's not useful for me.
Answer: Show them the referral videos or messages from previous customers. Tell them that even these customers did not believe in the product earlier. However, just as they have filmed a video recommending the product to others, the present prospective buyer will reap the benefits and be pleased after purchasing and utilising the things. I would like to mention a few more points here:

First, before beginning the sales discussion, please check the points pertaining to his financial status. How is his financial situation? Can he spend the money your product will entail? You can judge this while asking him questions about his family background and his occupation.

Second, you must check the authority and decision-making ability of the prospective buyer. Check the points as following:

- Is he empowered and authorized to buy?
- How senior is he in the hierarchy?
- Does he have a partner in business? This could be a friend or his wife. If he has a partner, it's better to request him to call them as well. It will save not only your time and effort, but it will also help the customer as he does not have to explain to others again.

Apart from these two crucial aspects, please check demographic factors. Suppose you are selling a course worth Rs 3,000 to a person who lives 30 km away and will have to travel every day, thereby spending Rs 5,000. Surely, he will not buy this course. But he can buy a significantly more value adding course, which may cost Rs 25,000. This is because now the value is greater than the cost of travelling. Psychologically, the new course may now make sense to him. This is similar to the situation in corporates when, while hiring a candidate, the hiring company asks questions pertaining to the candidate's current city and the feasibility of the candidate relocating, if needed.

People say that you should not debate with customers, but rather focus on selling. I always tell people that you should not even sell, you should coach customers to help them in their decision of selling. Coaching, education and spreading awareness are the keys.

The Art of Objection Handling

People may have different types of objections. You need to be ready to handle these. One customer asked me once, "Sir, why purchase the course now? I am 60 years old now. What benefit will I get by taking the course at this age?"

You can ask a few questions to the customer and make him reflect on his thinking. Some of the questions could be:

"Sir, what is the age of the Prime Minister of India?"

"Sir, at what age was Gandhi ji fighting the battle of freedom?"

"Sir, have you heard the story of the founder of KFC? Do you know at what age he opened his first KFC outlet?"

While answering these questions, he will realize that his notion is wrong and he can buy the course at any age.

You can also tell him the stories of oldest marathon runners and other such inspiring personalities.

I also say at times, "Sir, you have received a lot from the country while working till the age of 60. You have earned and settled the careers of your children. You have enjoyed your life, and of course you might have had your own share of challenges. Now, it's time for you to give back to society. In the game of cricket, batsmen hit the most in the last few overs. Instead, you are thinking of going silent in this crucial phase of your life. Sir, this is the right time to hit fours and sixes. This course will give you the perfect pitch and batting skills to live the most enjoyable and memorable inning of your life."

Suppose a customer says, "I am already the owner of a large corporation with Rs 100 crore. Your training company is a small one. How will that add value to my company?"

You can say, "Sir, you are the best person to know your company. But in our company, we have trainers who have been working with many companies of various sizes. This gives them a wide and unique knowledge base, which they can use to grow your company. While running your company, you get used to it and stop seeing the weak spots within it. But a third person can easily see weak spots and tell you about them. Hence, I am sure we will add value to your company."

You can also use challenging question as an opportunity to make the customer aware of some of the largest projects that you have completed. Maybe, the customer does not know much about the client base. You can say, "Sir, our training company is built on one foundation, and that is more than ours, we care for the size of your i.e., our customers' business. We have a list of many companies which have grown bigger and we are already a leading training company. We are growing bigger but as I said, it's about the size of our customers and not only about our size."

You should remember one point here; you need not be aggressive in your tone to convince your customers. You can be calm and composed while putting forth your points, and customers may like that as well. You do not have to shout or yell to impress the customers. A few people might be wondering whether they need to build a high level of energy like me. I always tell them, it's not needed. You can follow your personality style and practice all the tools that I am giving you. You can sell.

You have to practice selling every day for three months. You should work for 8-9 hours daily while handling 200-1000 objections. There will come a time when you will be smilingly waiting for new objections from the customer and there could be none as he has already exhausted all his objections and you have to answer to all his queries. You will know very soon that whatever it could be, you will hit a six on every new ball of objection you will be getting across. The funny thing is, there are hardly any objections beyond a set of 20-22. You just have to master answering them. In the movie, *Wolf*

Of Wall Street, the founder asks his salespeople about what kind of objections they are getting. He asks them to enlist all, and finds that all the salespersons are coming across a maximum of thirty objections.

Themore you practice handling live objections, the more confident you will become, at this. If you meet ten customers a day and handle their objections, you will easily handle manifold of these as well, only if you do this consistently. You will then be willing to handle any new objections as you will start enjoying the process which will become like a game where you come across the same set of objections most of the time.

"Good leaders ask great questions," wrote John Maxwell.

"Good salespersons ask great questions," I always say during seminars.

Chapter 8
Human Needs and Sales

People have six basic needs. You must understand these needs to be able to sell well. Sales, after all, is all about meeting the said and unsaid needs in a profitable way. The six basic human needs are as follows:

1. Need of Certainty: All human beings have the need of certainty. That means, they all want security or surety about their time and life. To understand it better, let me ask you this:

A person goes to a job for forty years in spite of not liking it because he knows that if he doesn't go to work, he will be uncertain about his life. The fear of uncertainty makes people do or not do certain things. And the love for certainty makes them behave positively.

When people are uncertain about relationships, they go for divorce; and when they are sure about the relationship, then they get married.

So why are we discussing this need here? Because when you are selling something to someone, you are actually passing that emotion of certainty to your customers.

For this, you must have conviction about your product and service.

Certainty is not just an emotion. It's a need which must be met at any cost, if you want to sell. The great news is that you can pass this on by the way you communicate and behave during the sales call. In sales, you must be extremely energetic. Only then can you guarantee your consumers' satisfaction. You demonstrate certainty by sharing recommendation tales with potential consumers. I give several real-life tales of business owners who have increased their profits after taking one of my courses.

2. Need of Variety: The next need of people is to have variety. Yes, variety is a need. We can't eat the same food every day. We can't follow the same routine every day. We can't laugh on the same joke again and again and we can't even watch the same movie every day. Why?

Because we love change. We want surprises. We love adventure. Suppose you already know the fate of a cricket match; would you ever watch that? A big no! Correct?

This is again a big need and every salesperson must address this during his sales call – how will the product or service make the customer feel differently or add massive value to his living standards?

How you can use this need for making more sales, might be a big question.

Here is the answer:

Make your customers imagine how your solutions and products will change their life. How they will feel. You also need to remind them how this life is going to be boring if they keep on using the same product.

Do you remember the ads of mountain dew or thumbs up? Yes "*Dar Ke Aage Jeet hai*" and "*Aaj kuch toofani karte hai*". Theyshow that how you will feel after drinking these beverages and maximum people want to feel that high, and they drink. Even though their logical mind knows that nothing of that sort is going to happen, but still they buy.

That's the power of the need of variety. You must learn to fulfil this need to ensure better results in your sales efforts.

3. Need of Significance: Every person whom you meet wants to feel special and significant. Majority of clashes and heartburns in families happen because of one reason; an unsatisfied ego. People have a high ego, of which no one in the family is taking care. Since they have an inherent need to feel special, which is not being fulfilled in the family, they go to extremes to make others feel their 'significance'. This leads to clashes, fights and even serious crimes in the family.

This is again the most important need and the customer must feel special during the sales call. A sales professional can meet this need by doing the following things during a sales call or before and after a sales call:

- You appreciate the customers and make them feel special to break the ice and they will instantly connect with you.
- You can take their permission before asking questions.
- You make them realize that they are your best customers.
- You listen to them very well.
- You paraphrase what they have spoken.
- You remind them about their achievements and their good points.
- You learn to use language in an effective way.
- You remember their birthdays and anniversaries and wish them.

- You always congratulate them for their every small and big achievements.

4. Need of Love/Connection: Everyone desires to obtain something more. I provide several courses to clients, many of them are very expensive. But whenever I ask people about their favourite programme, they mostly say in unison, Commando Training. This is because of only one reason; in Commando training, which is conducted in the early morning hours, I connect with people on a deeper level. As we do meditation, affirmations, gratitude or other such practices, I share my love and good vibes with them in early morning hours. A great beginning of the day makes the rest of the day happier and more energetic for people and that is how they remember this programme as their most favourite programme. Show love and connection with your customers and you will reap rich dividends. Show them that you truly care for them. Do not only talk about money. Talk about their well-being and how you can help them to be more successful.

5. Need of Growth: Everyone has a need to grow in life and career. People want to be better at what they are doing. They want an expansion in their capacity, capability and understanding. As a salesperson, you need to address this basic need of clients and show a clear connection between purchasing your product or service and their upcoming growth.

6. Need of Contribution: Everyone has a need to contribute to the society. It makes you happy. Think of the last time you went to an orphanage or an old age home and contributed some money or your time. Did you feel good or not? I am sure your answer will be in affirmation. This is because you fulfilled your need of contribution. You might have seen many companies telling you that a part of your money will go for some charity. It inspires you to make the buying decision. This is one of the needs of customers which you should keep in mind.

Sales and Unconsidered Needs

Sales is about serving the needs of the customers. But what is so great about it if you see that all the competitors are doing the same. Everyone is talking of the need and pains, if these are not met. Customers, in that case, decide to be in their comfort zone and do not reach out or respond to any of the sellers' calls or meetings.

But there is one way you can reach out to the customers and that is through serving the unconsidered needs. These needs are neither expressed by the customers nor catered by any of the competitors. We can utilize probing questions in this situation. We can inquire as to the true cause of the customer's distress. He will keep talking about the pains of his business and life. Let's have a look at the following conversation:

"Sir, what do you think are the reasons that your business is not growing?"

"My employees are the real reason. Theyare not putting their best. Also, suppliers keep troubling me…"

"Sir, do you think that all these external reasons will fall in place if you improve your personality and leadership style. Please do not mind, sir. I am just trying to help you figure it out and make your business profitable. Do you think your business is not growing because of your personality, which has remained weak and you are yet to work on it? Have you released your new version 2.0 or 3.0?"

In this conversation, you can easily understand how the unconsidered need of the customer is being brought to the forefront. Now, the chance for you to sell your course on 'Unconsidered Need' is higher and that the customer will buy it now. Till now, this was not even in the domain of discussion.

Consultative Selling

People do keep buying, but they do not like the idea that someone should sell you a product. Even if they are happy after buying, their friends and neighbours may ridicule them by saying, "Hey, who made you buy this product? You were sold and did not even realize. You are a fool..."

The salesperson must have high degree of pride on his/her products.

Let's talk about consultative selling. I always ask my sales team to go and meet customers as an educator and consultant and not as a person who is only looking for money.

Thetask of an educator is to listen to the problems of the customer and give them solutions.

I always listen to the problems of customers and provide them with solutions. And then, I help them take a decision.

Let me give an example here. Suppose you have to sell water bottles to a corporate client. You can tell him how by keeping 2-3 guards or pantry staff, the client is losing out on time and efficiency. His housekeeping staff is busy the whole day, while serving water to visitors. Instead of doing this, they can keep water bottles which are quick to grab, easy to drink and safe in the days of pandemic, as these are not touched by too many people. Also, it saves water as people can drink some water and preserve some for their further consumption. In the traditional way, people are served water in glasses and after taking a sip, the water goes to waste as you can't keep the glass on the table due to electronic gadgets there. Moreover, water bottles are safe on the table as water does not spill.

It's better to keep the required number of water bottles in all meeting rooms right in the morning and let the staff do some other, more productive work. You can also reduce the number of staff, if you want.

Such interactions, which make complete sense to the customers, are a part of consultative selling. You have to do the following as a part of consultative selling:

- Research about the customer
- Probing questions
- Deep listening (includes observing their body language)
- Questions to help him see the solution
- Questions and information to help him take a decision
- Show alternatives

Whenever we sell a big coaching programme worth lakhs of rupees, we do not force people to make an on-the-spot decision. It's an invisible service, not a tangible product. We listen to the customers, answer the problems, ask them relevant questions, and in essence, follow all six steps mentioned above as a part of consultative selling. As a part of selling a high-ticket coaching programme, we also suggest and gift some additional low ticket programmes like meditation courses, etc., to the customers. Then we advise customers to practice this over the next few days and think over his decision to come for the coaching programme. It's all about care, support, consultation and friendliness. Customers will appreciate the fact that you care for him and are willing to support him in his life and career. Then the sale happens in a mutually win-win situation.

More on Sales and the need of Certainty

Till 2-3 years ago, I used to have a turnover of Rs 2-3 crore only. In the last financial year, I set a goal of attaining a turnover of Rs 10 crore and attained a turnover of 9.3 crore. This gap of around 70 lakhs was only to the fact that our team could not follow up with clients. This was primarily because of a few courses for which I ask the customers to pay only a fraction of the fee in the beginning and the remaining fee can be paid later on. We could not follow-up with the customers after a few months and hence this gap. Or else, we would have met our target.

For the next financial year, I have set a goal of Rs 100 crore, which is ten times this year's sales.

If you have conviction in your goals and certainty of purpose, sales is the most certain profession. Here, the results are always in black and white and with a clarity of thoughts, you can create magic.

Once you set a goal, you must do the reverse calculation or else you will not be able to attain your goals.

Wondering what is reverse calculation?

Think of a wedding which has been scheduled a month later. The family does all kinds of reverse calculations before the wedding and decides on different actions on different dates, keeping a budget for all actions.

When will the clothing be purchased?

How many people are needed to be invited? When and where the cards will be printed?

Which hotel needs to be booked and at what rate?

Which party needs to be fixed for arranging flowers and for decorations?

How many vehicles shall we need and at what cost?

And then you plan while doing reverse calculation.

Similarly, if I have set a goal of Rs 100 crore, I need to plan different actions under different verticals against different revenues and reach the goal of Rs 100 crore.

Let's take the example of a factory which wants to sell 600 machines in the current year before 31st Dec 2023. How many prospects do they need to target assuming that one customer normally buys one machine? Here are the numbers as per the methodology of reverse calculation.

- 6,000 prospects, if you are a good salesperson assuming a conversion/hit rate of 10%
- 12,000 prospects if you are an average salesperson with a conversion ratio of 5%
- 24,000 prospects in you are a below-average salesperson with a conversion ratio of 2.5%

Now, if you are a team of a hundred people, all that you have to do is to make every team member set a presentation to 60, 120 or 240 prospects depending on the skill level of your sales team.

Every member should maintain a diary or goal tracker. They should update the tracker every day, just like a cricket score board is updated with every ball. They should know the 'asking run rate'. Sales is a matter of goals and review of progress.

This will give you the sales of 600 machines. Remember, as I have mentioned elsewhere in the book, sales follows the law of averages. The more the prospecting; the more the sales. Even the best of salespersons have an upper cap on conversion. There is a chance for every type of salesperson – excellent, average or below average!

When you transfer your emotion to the minds of your customers, you make a sale.

When I sell, I transfer the confidence and conviction which I have about my courses into the minds of clients, and only then the process of sales will be completed.

I conduct seminars on sales and various other topics and people travel from hundreds and thousands of kilometres. But why do they do so when many of them might not even have travelled a few kilometres to attend a wedding in their city? They do so for one reason. I have been able to transfer the conviction and enthusiasm about the course from my heart to theirs.

Let's look at the way of transferring the certainty to someone else.

Think of ways to transfer your confidence to someone else.

First factor is – **trust**. You need to build trust in the mind of the customer to make him believe in your conviction.

Think of the pandemic days. The worst times are the best opportunities to grow. In the days of Covid, when most of the people suffered, there were few who through their self-conviction, grew their business.

I am a motivational speaker, business coach and author and have seen one common trend. People who are best connected with me are the ones I speak to in their times of distress. People who are at the rock bottom in their life and are struggling to survive, value my programmes the most and those who do not have any hunger to excel may actually appear indifferent to me and my programmes.

Sales is such a profession which can make a man Osama or Obama, depending on which salesperson met them. Someone transferred his/her confidence into the mind of Obama that the latter can do the extreme by becoming the President of the USA. Some other salesperson transferred his confidence to Osama that by creating havoc in the world, the latter would directly find a place in heaven and be endowed with blessings and all the luxuries of life. Osama in turn sold this conviction to people so well that people became ready to lay their lives by crashing planes they flew.

This is the power a salesperson can bring for both negative and positive reasons. Here of course we are talking about the positive way of selling.

Let me tell you a story of a person who once lived in a village.

Whenever I sell a course from the stage to masses, I ask a question towards the end, just before selling; "If you make Fixed Deposit of the same amount which you have paid me for my programme and get 100% return per year, how many people will deposit their money in the FD? Then I ask another question, "If you make Fixed Deposit of Rs 1 lakh and will get an assured return of Rs 25 lakhs after ten years, how many people will make the FD?" Now imagine if the second offer/assurance is given by State Bank of India, would you invest your money on the same day? I am sure the answer in most of the cases could be a yes as it's SBI, a highly trusted name behind the assurance. However, if the first assurance is given to you by a bank which is not trustworthy, there won't be any deal.

It's all about the certainty of the offer and certainty of the offer-giver which matter the most.

Always remember a point – Sales is not selling; it's recovering.

Hence, you need to have a process of following-up and recovering your money from the customers.

There has got to be a creative way to recover your money. Think of the example of Kinley, a brand of drinking water. Who would have thought till a few years ago that someone will sell bottled drinking water someday! After all, drinking water was supposed to be a given. Not only are people today buying drinking water bottles, they are also ready to pay more than Rs 3 lakhs for a machine which makes drinking water.

So much business and selling around a commodity as simple as drinking water! Hence, if you can be slightly creative, you can sell anything you strongly believe in.

Do you recall one very important aspect of becoming a strong salesperson? It is your belief and conviction in your product/coach/speaker which matters the most.

If you are convinced about your product, it will show the customer and then they will buy it with happiness and excitement.

It's always about you and not about a few others who you think are either not supporting you or you are conducting the view himself.

You should give such high degree of certainty to the customer that he should be begging to buy the product from you. The customer will do so only if he gets certainty. I often tell the participants of my seminars that they are here with me in a conference room of a good hotel due to the following certainties (of course they have bought from me because of these certainties only. They are my clients):

- Their family is certainly good and safe back home
- They will certainly learn something from me in the conference
- They will certainly not contract Corona in the conference room

They have paid money to join my conference only because they have a sense of certainty of benefits which they will get from my programme. This means, I have taken efforts to give them certainty about me and my programmes.

Importance of Value Creation in Sales

Whenever you are selling your product, you should create value for your product and company in the mind of the customer. You can do so while addressing the basic human needs of the customer. There are three requirements of creating value and these are as follows:

1. Whatever value you are sharing with the customer should be very unique and different from that of your competitors. For example, product dimension, safety, service, or quality could be of value to the customer. The value should be differentiating. Example: 'Thums Up' gives the message of 'taste the thunder'. If you drink Thums Up, you will do something thunderous and adventurous. The messages of Coca Cola and Pepsi are different than this. Every brand has a unique message. In a country like India, where every city has some unique and delicious sweets, Cadbury has been hammering the minds of people with the idea that whenever there is a good occasion, you should eat chocolates and nothing else. Many Indian sweet shops have been struggling because of the marketing campaigns of Cadbury, which have been driving a unique value to customers by creating colourful and shining

packets and making them easy to buy and carry. And of course, it also tastes good and is easily available everywhere.

2. The value should be important to the customers. Your offering may be unique, but if it is not important to the customer, it will not sell. 'Thums Up' marketing team knows that a sense of adventure is important for a certain segment of customers. Hence, they pitch their product in the garb of adventure and excitement. Human beings love being adventurous and leading an exciting life, and hence Thums Up's value is important for them.

3. You have to give proof of the value you claim your product will offer the customer. So how do I give proof? Thebest way is to give evidence or testimonials to the customers. Gather testimonial videos and write-ups from current and past customers and share them with future consumers as proof of the value you provide through your products and services. You can also provide proof through some research data. You can share the data on your happy customers.

You have to keep practicing these three things till the customer buys the products. In other words, you have to keep doing these three till you close sale with the customer.

Chapter 9
Sales models and Techniques

Wow! Massive learnings in all these chapters so far. Now we are on the final chapter. Hurray!

I am trying to make the book very easy for all of you, but to be very honest – Sales is deep. Few people with great intellect and common sense can pick this fast and few take a lifetime and still can't master it. But I believe you, and I am sure you will understand the power of this massive skill and will use it for the betterment of your customers and yourself.

In this final chapter, we will look into the models and technique which you should study carefully, practice in real life and master them. These techniques are very powerful and you will master these with practice and yes, some more practice.

Sales and Spin Selling Model

SPIN model is a crucial model which is based on asking questions. It's an acronym which stands for the following:

- Situation
- Problem
- Implication

- Need pay off

In the first stage, you ask questions related to the situation. You can ask the following questions:

- How is your business doing?
- How do you plan to grow the business?
- What supports do you think you will require to attain your goals?
- How does the market of your products look in near future?

While the customer explains these, your next step should be to ask questions related to the problems. You can ask the customer to tell you more about the kind of problems which the customer is facing. These questions are vital as these will give you an idea of the kind of your products which will fit in here.

Then you can talk about the implication of not taking any action. Let the customers know how they are going to suffer if they let the status quo continue. For example, if I am selling my morning commando training programmes, I need to tell customers how by not doing anything to increase their energy and focus on their day-to-day routine matters, they are losing ground to competitors or others around them. If they do not awaken the hidden powers of their mind, they will continue to live the same boring and lack luster life of failures and heartbreaks.

Coming to need pay off, ask questions on what kind of benefits the customer may get. Let the customers share the pay-off which his investment will give him. While telling you the benefits, he is actually thinking of the benefits. This is a more active way of thinking that is more effective than simply educating clients about the benefits. This increases the likelihood of a customer purchasing your goods or service.

Technique to approach a customer in Sales

Every salesperson adopts a unique approach of selling. At a generic level, there are four sales approaches as follows:

- Premium (give a small portion free)
- Product (make them experience a slice of the product)
- Network (Referral and reference-based approach)
- Prescriptive

I use premium sales approach just like a few other coaches do. In this, we sell our products to customers who are sitting on the fence. They are not aware of their needs. They may actually need a product or course, but they are blinded towards the need. They are indecisive. So, what we do is offer a free course to such customers. We can give a scratch coupon to a customer who visits a mall. Or, the customer can get a small pack of candies or ice cream the next time he visits the mall. The customer finds it harmless in trying a scratch coupon. I conduct free webinars. Hence, many people including the fence sitters become curious to attend my webinars. They do not have any idea of what I am going to speak about in the webinar. Customers come just like that and then after hearing me, get a good idea about my products or courses. And they are more likely to try and purchase one of the courses or products.

Coming to product experience, when you enter a showroom for lifestyle related products in a mall, and go to the perfume section, you may find some salespersons making you experience a particular perfume free of cost. They will spray it on your wrist so that you can smell and experience the perfume. Here, there is no free coupon; it's a free product experience. When you go to a car showroom and the salesperson takes you for a free ride in the car, it again falls in the same category. It's all about real experience and no free coupon etc., which you actually may or may not test.

In the network-based approach, you build connections. You keep meeting people. You teach them something and learn something from them. You build a network and then can generate referrals. One of the guys in your network will actually tell someone else in his network to buy your product. Related to this is reference selling, where the customer gives you some references. Here, the customer does not talk about you or your product to others; he gives the contacts, and you actually do the talking and the rest of the work to convert the prospect into a buyer. Hence, under the network-based sales approach, you have both *referral* and *reference* based selling approach.

In prescriptive selling, a salesperson understands the problem of the customer and prescribes a few possible solutions. Less is the number of solutions, better it is, as it does not confuse the customer. I personally suggest that only one solution be suggested. If you are selling more products, the customer will either get confused or buy the cheapest product. Hence, I suggest only one target product or course to the customer at a time.

You can use a mix of all these approaches and your sales will improve for sure.

3 Ts in sales

There are 3 Ts in sales which go like this:

1. Teach customers
2. Tailor your talk
3. Take control of the discussion/situation

You need to teach customers on the features and benefits of the products. You need to teach customers on how they are losing on an opportunity by ignoring your product offering and how their life will be transformed forever if they take your products.

You also need to tailor your talk as per the preference and needs of the customer. You need to take control of the situation. You need to practice these three without letting the customers know of it. Every consumer is unique, as are their demands and problem points. There is no such thing as a one-size-fits-all solution. You must adapt your approach, which can only happen if you have done some preliminary work before meeting the customer. Lastly, you need to take control of the situation in the course of the sales conversation. There has to be only one person in command of the situation in the entire course of selling, from beginning of the call or the meeting till the end of discussion and closure of sale, and that is you.

Remember these three Ts of sales and practice them in your sales conversations.

The Sandler sales method

Most of the times, we ask the customers to purchase our products and services. Imagine a situation which is just the reverse. Instead of you impressing upon the customers to buy your products, the customer is asking you to sell the products to him and you are least bothered or desperate to sell. If you can bring forth such a situation, sale becomes even easier.

So, what do you do in Sandler's sales method?

You identify the problem of the customer, explain the features of the products or services and show him how your product or service will meet his need. Then comes the funny part, which is purely a matter of psychology.

Now, when the customer wants to buy your products, you actually tell the customer not to buy the product. Yes, you read it correctly – you actually dissuade the customer from making the buying decision.

You will tell your customers that the product is only for those customers who want a complete transformation in their life. This product has made many customers super rich and successful, but you should not purchase it if you are not yet ready for it. It needs a high degree of commitment and if you do not feel committed for it, don't go for it.

I can give a personal example of this kind of selling. While selling our commando training programme, we tell our customers clearly that if they are not disciplined enough to get up at 4:30 in the morning, they should not invest in the programme. We tell them – we are not interested in their money; instead, we are interested in their discipline. Only those who can join us early in the morning should buy the programme. The funny thing is – our team gets daily calls and follow up from people who request to buy the programme not only for them, but also for their whole family. We have 3,000 people joining us at the same time during commando training.

This is the power of Sandler's method of selling.

To recapitulate, this method includes three steps before you dissuade customers to buy:

1. Technical Details
2. The Business/Financial impact
3. Disqualify/dissuade customer

In case of hotels, the salesperson will tell you that a lower category room is available at a higher price and he cannot give you any better room. You ask for a better room. Then the salesperson says that he has to talk to the superior. Then he comes back to you saying that he cannot give a better room but can give complimentary breakfast. You will happily agree for the same room which he was offering earlier for the same high price as you sensed a chance of disqualification by the salesperson. This is one of the examples of the Sandler's method of selling.

Price Uncertainty

While you need to create certainty about the product by not selling multiple products across different price points at the same time, you must create price uncertainty to get quick and more sales. Some of the ways to create price uncertainty are as follows:

"This price is valid only till today. Prices are not the same and will rise by a minimum of 50% by tomorrow. The same product which is being offered at a price of Rs 4999 today will be available at no less than Rs 8,000 tomorrow."

"We are offering ten bonuses along with the product today. These bonuses will not be available if you don't buy the product today."

"Prices keep on moving up and down. This is the best price which I can offer and it is valid only till today."

"I reward action taker and hence price is the lowest at Rs 3,999 only for today. If you buy it in the next fifteen minutes, you will get it at this price or else the price will be reset to Rs 5499 after fifteen minutes. Take quick action and get rewarded."

You might be wondering – what will happen if I allow twenty-four hours or more to prospective customers so that they can think through and take a well thought out decision? Well the answer is that be sure that out of the customers who promised to revert in the next 24 hours, only 20% will actually do. Hence, if your target was to sell worth five lakh rupees, you will actually be selling worth only one lakh. This is the kind of dip in sales you will see if you do not keep price uncertainty or allow too much time to customers.

Planning an Efficient Sales Meeting

You need to plan before going for a sales meeting. Let's look at the ways to plan a sales meeting in the following different types of meeting:

B2C meetings: In case you are going for a sales meeting with an individual, keep testimonials ready as the customer needs to build trust on you. Keep some visuals ready with you or some of the programmes which you have conducted in case you are going to speak about those. Keep some certificates with you. You may also carry the registration proof with some government offices as a testimonial. Few letters of appreciation from past customers will also help. You may also keep some newsletter clippings in case you were featured in some magazine or journals. Customer success or transition stories are also important. You should keep anywhere between ten to a hundred success stories of customers with you, depending on how many years you have been in the field. This is an extremely important step for building customers' trust. You can make a folder to keep all of these. You should also keep your offers ready with you.

You should keep your presentation ready with you.

In case of tele-calling, a script is written by experts and followed by the sales callers. A sales script is always a great idea. I have worked in an IT BPO company and have personally used these scripted sales calls. These are typically helpful in building rapport with the customer before you actually discuss the actual products, service or issues.

You may also carry a demo product, if needed.

Objection handling is another important area you should be prepared before planning a sales meeting.

Another thing you should plan before a sales meeting is planning for your time. This is important so that you reach the customer on or before time.

Planning for place and accessories is also important. Many a times, I do sales from the stage and hence I may require a whiteboard, flip chart, etc.

You should also carry a diary and pen as it, apart from giving a positive message to the customer that you are noting down his queries and points, also makes it easy for you to remember the points later on.

You should be presentable. You should wear decent clothes. In case you are travelling in a place like Rajasthan, where its hot and sweaty, you should carry some deodorants, etc., so that you appear more presentable in front of the customer.

Planning an Online Sales Meeting

You need to know a few things for an online sales meeting. Here is a list:

- **Camera:** You need to check your camera for cleanliness and clarity.
- **Mic:** Check your mic.

- **Control:** You need to check all features which you are going to use. You need to have all controls under you.
- **Internet connection:** Always keep a few backups of dongles, hotspots, etc. so that in case your primary source of connectivity (Wi-Fi, etc.) is not working, you can quickly switch over to back up sources.
- **Light and electricity:** You may say that there is no electricity failure in your area. I say – don't take any sales meeting for granted. You need to keep a power back up.
- **Laptop and charger:** Your laptop and mobile phones should be fully charged. At times, if power goes off for whatever reason, if you have a fully charged laptop, you can have an uninterrupted meeting.
- **Background noise:** Keep a good environment from the place you are going to conduct the online meeting. There should not be any background noise.
- **Organizing documents:** You need to keep all your testimonials and presentation files in place so that you can show them immediately when asked for or needed. You should have practiced the usage of whiteboard, recording software, etc., so that you are at ease while using these documents or software tools.

- **Time:** You should always finish your meeting within time. Customers may not interrupt you out of courtesy, but it leaves a bad impression. Hence, keep a check on time.

Sales Meeting – Conclusion

Different sales calls may require different types of preparations. For example, if you working in a network marketing company, you can hire an auditorium. Or else, if you have to give awards, you can advise these people in advance. You may need external vendors to manager light, sound or stage. Your team may be requested to plan ahead of time for this. Similar arrangements can be trained for your team. A sales encounter should never be taken for granted. Every call should be taken as a new call with preparation. You never know – you may get a well-prepared customer who may ask new questions. Prepare your mind and your body. Be ready as the customer this time might not even have heard about you.

Specific care in case of Corporate or Institutional Selling

If you are making a sales pitch to corporate veterans or IAS officers, you need not follow the agreement frame questions or directional questions. They are senior people who have attained a certain level in their career and will not even allow you to ask these questions. In these cases, you need to be confident and patient. Here, one sale can give you the outcome worth a hundred sales in case of other retail clients. Many corporates have a large number of factories and if they are convinced about one product, they can place orders for many factories and it could be a large order volume.

In case of corporates and big clients, you should follow the rule of 3-3-3-3, meaning thereby, approach three new customers, follow up with three customers, send three proposals and hold three meetings every day. Follow this for the next ninety days and you will see results coming up.

Reference and Referrals in Sales

Whenever you learn about sales, it's a must to know about reference and referrals. You can get sales while smiling and laughing with customers if you master these two words.

Picture this - You have spent some good time while working with a prospect and have converted him into a happy customer. You have spent a long time while doing this and now the customer is happy with your product, services or a course. Can he help you gain more customers? Absolutely yes! Let's learn how.

You can ask the customer for references or referrals.

If the customer gives you a few names and contacts and asks you to connect with them, its known as a reference. You have to connect with the customers yourself, but there is a slight advantage as you can always tell the customer that you have got the reference from one of his friends or someone he knows.

In referral, selling becomes even easier as the customer himself makes a call to one of his friends or companions and tells him how effective your products or services are. He gives his personal example of how happy he is and then you meet the potential customer separately. But in this case, selling becomes even easier than it was in case of reference. By the time you meet the potential customer, he always knows about your product features and price, etc. You do not even have to negotiate on price etc., most of the times.

Use reference and referrals to sell more.

Let's talk a bit more about reference now. You must take reference from as many customers as possible. The best time to seek reference from the customer is to ask when he has already paid money and that means the customer has already taken the decision to buy and has also happily paid for this. This is the best time when the customer is happy and will be happy giving references.

Say something like this – "Congratulations sir for buying this product. It's a great one and you have taken the right decision. Sir, can I also request you to share 3-5 references if you are happy with the product. I will be happy speaking with them separately. Also, sir, can you please send an SMS or make a call to the references from your end. It will help me when I speak with them later."

You can also ask customer a few questions about the references. For example, you can check whether the references will be financially ready to buy now. You can ask when it would be okay for you to make a call to them – now or later.

You should also be ready for a question from the customers – "What will I get if I refer a few customers to you and you get the order?" Some customers may also ask this question. You can give an offer that in such a case, 20% of the order value will be paid to the customer. To give my example, I have launched 'Learn and Earn programme' under which people who refer my programmes to their relatives, friends or colleagues, etc., and there is a sale, 'Learn and Earn partners' get a certain % of the sale value. This is a win-win-win model as the customers get a good programme, people who refer earn money and I also get a sale done. Ultimately, every partner in the process of sales is getting benefitted.

Now, let's take our discussion on referrals a little forward. In the previous paragraph, we discussed reference a bit. Referrals are even more powerful a tool of sales. One of your customers has spoken about the goodness of your product to one of his acquaintances. Now you have to approach the customer who already knows that your product is good. Today's economy is an experience-based economy. If customers have a good experience, they refer your products to other potential customers and that is how the sales progress. In case of referral, you need to have the confidence of giving a good product and service to the potential customer if you get the order. This is because the prestige of your customer who has given the referral is at stake. If you do not give a good experience to the new customer, the earlier customer who has given the referral is going to be unhappy and there may not be any further referrals going forward.

In case of referrals, speed is the key and hence you need to approach the new potential customer at the earliest. This is because your existing customer has just now spoken with the potential customer and given the referral of your product. It's your duty to reach out to the potential customer without any delay.

Always remember that the selling efforts in case of a referral sales is only 25% of the original effort and hence you should be fast, courteous and efficient in handling such sales cases.

Sales and Importance of Publicity:

The biggest problem in the life of a salesperson is that many people do not even know that the salesperson is present in the market and is selling a certain product or service. It's important to market yourself shamelessly. If you need to expand the market, you need to create visibility and trust. Till a few years ago, I never liked putting my pictures on the stage. I never liked putting my pictures everywhere I held my shows. I never liked putting my pictures on social media.

Then I realized the problem.

The problem was – I was shameful of keeping my displays at too many places. The day I decided to be visible and keep my well-designed pictures and standees everywhere, I saw the change happening. Customers started recognizing me as a person who had to offer something on a consistent basis. I slowly came out of obscurity.

"That which is not visible, does not sell," you must have heard.

Why do Coca Cola and Pepsi sell?

Why do burgers and French fries sell?

Do people not know that these are junk foods without any nutritious value?

People know all of this and still they consume these junk foods, which do not have goodness within. Instead, these products lead to serious ailments.

It's only because whatever is visible, you purchase, even if it is not good for you many a time.

This is the only reason you keep seeing almost the same or similar ads of cola and junk food. The marketeers just want you to keep seeing these and that generates brand recall in your mind.

You must make a promise to yourself that if you meet twenty customers today, you must be visible to them forever.

Read the above sentence again – You should keep coming in touch with new customers and once you meet a new customer, they should see you regularly on social media as well as in real life. Your videos, pictures, emails, programmes, live sessions – these must keep happening.

Jo dikhta hai, wahi bikta hai…

Trust building techniques

Rapport building comes through many ways, including showing few past success stories. For example, if a customer tells me his problem and is wondering how my course will help him in overcoming these problems, I can tell him the stories of many existing customers who had even more serious problem and came out of those after taking the course. That will give him confidence as our society extrapolates past successes and hence, we need to show some past success stories.

Hence, building trust is one tool which will make the process of sales easy and smooth for you. What customers are looking for is trust. They want to know you and believe in your abilities. Once you build trust, you don't have to do hard sale. The process of building trust is time consuming and difficult, but it yields rich dividends on a long-term time horizon.

Let me cite an example – I have invested a minimum of Rs 60 lakhs for my two seasons of 'Magic of Thinking Rich' workshops. These workshops continued for twenty-eight days for one hour every day. In the first season, I conducted all the sessions myself. In the second season, I invited a new guest in each session for a month. I spent huge money on marketing and promoting both the events so that I could reach out to a large audience. Thousands of people joined me every day and over a period of time, they knew what I was capable of. They trusted me. Then when I launched my subsequent courses,

I saw a huge response and people started purchasing tickets to my live shows and my online courses in larger numbers. Today, I have become a brand which sells easily. No more hard selling. Let me cite an example.

After conducting two seasons of 'Magic of Thinking Rich', I launched a programme on 'Digital Course Academy' and within forty-eight hours, we had 750 people registering for the course. In the earlier days, if 2,000 people joined my webinar, hardly 40-50 people registered for the course. Now, we had 750 people registering with the same efforts. It only had one meaning – people had started trusting me and my brand now.

I know, I have a long way to go on the journey of building even more trust, but one thing is for sure – with efforts and investments to build your brand, you come to a stage where people purchase courses just by hearing your name.

Some of my trainees tell me – "Sir, please teach us some way so that we don't have to do door to door selling. I don't want to convince every individual."

My advice to you is to conduct webinars and find ways to reach out to 5,00-1,000 people in a quarter and you will earn Rs 2 lakh per month on an average. Some of you might earn Rs 10,000 and some others may earn Rs 5 lakhs but on an average, you will most likely earn Rs 2 lakhs per month.

In Sales, only results matter

There are many good sales people who will explain all features of the products well and build rapport with the customer. They will build trust, but still they are not able to sell and get money.

Let me give an example from my team. A few of my sales team members used to work on filling the seminar halls by selling tickets of a programme, which was a low-ticket seminar. Theyused to visit many customers, explain the unique benefits of the programme and ask them to join. Many customers used to say that they will surely join the seminar. But actually, very few turned up. Instead of our target of 300 people, hardly 80-100 people used to turn up. When asked, my sales team used to say that they had put in their best. How could they help if their customers had promised to come and at the last minute they did not turn up? I finally had to call all my sales team members to Pune and conduct a sales training programme for them. I asked them a basic question – "How could I sell my Business Coaching programmes for Rs 2.5 lakh and they could not even sell low ticket programmes worth Rs 200 – 500?" I made them realize that the problem was not with the customer. It was with the selling skills of my team members.

I taught them that sales did not mean the number of hours put into the work. It meant closure and money received. It meant target-oriented work. It meant smart work and meeting revenue targets.

Let me take my personal example. If my training was not powerful enough to bring results for my clients, how could my team members muster energy and confidence to sell my products? Just like results matter for me, it also mattered for my team members. It's a result driven world and sales is no different.

In the following cycle, you can see that the cycle of sales should go on with more references received from a satisfied customer and more sales being closed. Thecycle should be repeated again and again. People feel that once you receive money, deliver products or service and get feedback from the customer, the process of sales comes to an end. No! the process of sales is not complete. It should lead to more sales with more references and more closures.

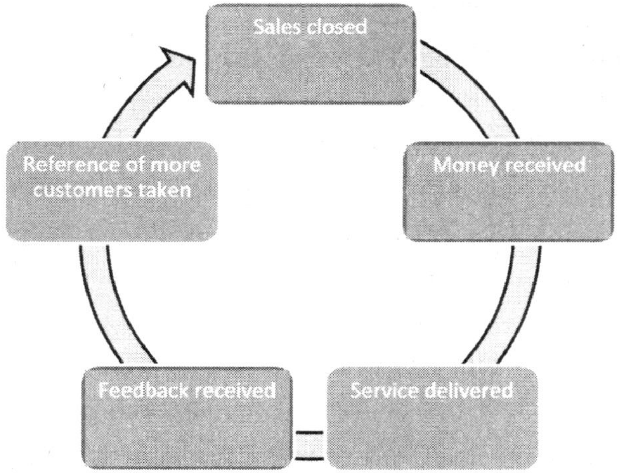

Types of sales closing techniques

Let's look at various types and techniques of sales closings.

1. **High Pressure closing:** You build high pressure on your potential clients for sales closure. This is typically done on customers who are known to you. One of my happy customers did this for some of his friends who were running a loss-making business. He cajoled his friends into buying my courses as he knew that unless his friends made some changes in the way they were running their business, they would not be able to pay. His friends resisted initially, saying that they did not have money to pay the salary. My customer said – "I know, you won't make money unless you take up this course. If you can't pay, I will give the cheque partially. I know it's the need of the hour for you. You should give the cheque

now and register for the course. There is no tomorrow for this…" Such a process of closing is known as High Pressure closing. The focus is always on closing the sale now.

2. **Comparison closing:** Here you give the example of another customer who has already purchased your product or service. You can talk about the benefits which the other customer is also getting. This gives confidence to the potential customer to make the buying decision and it helps you in closing the process of sales. You can also give examples of friends and competitors of your potential customer, who are making good money and doing better business than the person you are talking to. You show them a picture where they are losing ground in comparison with their friends who are making more profit, driving better cars and living in bigger houses. They are living a significantly better life. Then the prospective customer thinks of bridging the gap by buying the course or product. This is based on basic human psychology of comparing their success with others and be better than them.
3. **Compromise selling:** It's a selling where you compromise a bit to close the sales. I won't recommend this type of closing unless for a strategic or long-term measure, you think of yielding your ground a bit and still earn the customer. You know it's a high-profile customer with a potential business in future and hence you give some discount or extra benefits to attract the customer.
4. **Silence closing:** In this, you tell all that you wanted to convey. Now, you are silent. That silence says to the customer – "Now over to you. Decide and close the sale now." This is applied with certain customers who do not like negotiation and you want to

let them think and decide in that very moment. You can take a break and then again add to what you were saying earlier before going in silence again.

5. **Reverse closing:** Think of the closing technique of LIC agents. Theywill speak of the pain the customer's family will suffer from if something goes wrong with the customer. Here, you can say things like – "Sir, imagine what will happen if you do not purchase the product. You will remain where you are, mired with problems and pains. Your problems will keep multiplying..." Here, you show the extremely sad picture to the customer in case he does not make the buying decision.
6. **Barter closing:** As the name suggests, you give something else to the customer to get the order for your products or services. For example, I sold my courses to customers saying that they would get 20-25 customers from my community which I have built after hard work for twenty years. Such customers buy my courses and gain access to my client base to sell their products.
7. **Philosophical closing:** Here you tell stories and give examples from mythological texts and history. You compare the decisions taken by personalities from history and show to the customer how beneficial this decision could be. You tell stories and convince the customer on a philosophical basis.

A few sales people also follow a different approach of insult-based closing. Theywill make the customers feel insulted. Either the customer will buy or he will turn hostile. The basic philosophy is – only value those customers who pay money. Other customers do not matter to me. The world will anyway hate me. So why not focus on those customers who pay and get my products. This is the way of only a few sales people and the risk here is – you build an ever-growing community of people who do not like you.

Offers are important for closing

Sales closure becomes easy with a good offer. It does help in closing sales. You may not require it only in case you have a strong brand. A company like Apple may not need offers because they already have built a strong brand. But mostly companies need to make an offer to get sales closure.

Without getting into too much of details, let me cite a personal example. I was in the final stage of buying a house. However, negotiations were still going on. The broker made the following offer – "Sir, if we finalize the deal today, I will take care of all maintenance charges for the next ten years. Any kind of water or electricity problems will be upon us for the next decade. You are a well-known personality and this deal will add to our brand value. Hence, we are making this offer only for you."

In this offer, he had two messages – hassle free living for next ten years and a sense of exclusivity for me. Now you know how and why an offer makes sense. It should not come out of desperation; instead, it should come out of a positive interest to help the customer close a deal. After all, any purchasing must include the fun of shopping. When you go to a mall and do shopping, you have fun. Isn't it? Hence, it's important to make an offer to make the customer happy while closing sales.

Look around on Amazon, Swiggy, Uber and malls in your city. You will find offers all around you. Make it a habit to look for these offers, which are on a range of products from burgers to cars.

Let me share with you one powerful sales closing technique.

Suppose a customer is not willing to buy your product, course or idea citing lack of money as a reason. You can simply ask him a question – "What do you think will be your loss if you come for this programme? What would be the worst loss that you can think of?"

He may say – "... the worst loss could be the loss of money. Or else I don't think of any other loss ..." You can also guide him as you also know there is no other loss in the worst-case scenario. "And what else would you be losing ... ?" You may ask. He may think over and say – "... time which I will invest ..."

Here, you can show him 4-5 stories of your past mentees or customers who have transformed their life and have won big time. You can tell the client that you have many such stories of people who have won and nobody has lost. He will get confidence (he may not tell you about these though ...) after seeing the past success stories. Then you can tell him – "Sir, coming to the second possible area of loss, tell me one area of growth where you don't invest time. Let's take the example of stock trading or investment in shares. Do you think you don't have to work after investing the money? I can assure you that if you invest money and forget for next few years, your money will become nothing. Even if you give the money to someone else and ask him to invest, I can assure you that you have to keep a constant eye or else if you check the progress after a few years, your money would have gone. You always have to invest your time. Here, we also know that your time and money – both are investments and not expenses or cost and will surely fetch you results ..."

Now, let me tell you the gains which you can make and these are going to be life/career/business transforming. It's just one life and the biggest benefit will be that you will discover a ten times bigger life and money. Return will be 100-1000 times... Now compare and decide for yourself how the benefits look like in comparison with the loss..."

Most likely, the customer is planning to buy right away. You sparked his cognitive process and assisted him in overcoming some of the mental roadblocks that were inhibiting him from making the appropriate decision. Closure is crucial in sales. Most of the sales people will find it easy to complete all steps of sales except closing and getting the money. Here, offer based closing comes in very handy. It is said that people do not buy 'products', they buy an 'offer'. Offer creates FOMO or 'Fear of Missing Out'. Think of a customer who is in no hurry to purchase. Why should he be in hurry if he knows he can always buy later after a few months or weeks. Offer inspires him to purchase now as he will save money or get additional benefits if he buys now. You can offer the following:

- Discount if sales happens now
- Additional products or courses
- Money back guarantee

If, for example, we sell a product of online Sales Brahmastra for Rs 5,000, we include additional fifteen courses to give more value to the customer. When people see so many benefits for just Rs 5,000, they will think of purchasing now.

Asking for and securing token amount as a mark of completion of sales is important. You should keep respect, love and friendliness separate from asking for money. In a world of broken promises where people hardly keep their promises and turnaround from their words in a day, please make it a habit to ask for token amount. Do not hesitate form enforcing customers to pay on spot. Ask them to pay a token amount in case they express their inability to pay the full amount. My experience says that in case of low-ticket items, once a customer pays the token amount, 100% of them join the programme. In case of high-ticket item, 90% of people come for the programme and make the full payment.

Token amount is important for closure of sales because unless money changes pockets or accounts, there is always a high chance for the customer to change his mind as an afterthought. This keeps both the sales person and the customer in doubt.

You have noted in the above example that success stories are crucial in convincing customers from a variety of areas.

Sales closure means, you need to handle objections in a manner the client can connect with it. For example, if a customer says that he is in IT company and is not sure how your programme will help him. You should give a story of success from the field of IT. If someone says that he is from the field of business and he does not know how your programme will help him in his business, you should have a ready example of success of a businessman. You should have a success story for every customer matching his requirement. This means – you must have 100s of success stories which will enable you choose one of the stories of success which you think the customer will connect with.

Hence create as many success stories as possible and surely you need to have a minimum of a hundred success stories as a rule of thumb.

Multiple sources of income

You need to open all possible sources of income which are in sync with your belief system. No income is small till it matches your belief system and has the potential to grow in future. Let me take an example.

Positivity is a part of my belief system. Hence, if blockchain or any new source of income falls in the domain of my belief system, I may consider going for it. But I will not go for a source of income which may come from the trading of alcoholic beverages, for example.

Conclusion

In the grand tapestry of success, we often find ourselves standing at the crossroads of opportunity and uncertainty. Sell and Grow Rich is a profound journey that has unveiled the secrets to unlocking unlimited potential, transforming dreams into reality, and ascending to new heights of wealth and fulfillment.

Through these pages, we have explored the art and science of salesmanship, revealing the power of persuasion and the importance of building genuine connections. We have witnessed the birth of legends, the triumphs of visionaries, and the boundless rewards that await those who dare to step into their true potential. Now, armed with this knowledge, it is your turn to embrace the path of abundance, forever altered by the principles and wisdom contained within these sacred pages.

The world awaits your mastery, your brilliance, and your unyielding resolve to Sell and Grow Rich.

Connect with us

Connect with my team for more learnings on the journey.

You can contact us on our official email ID: contact@coachbsr.com

Or call our helpline number at 9667674477

To stay updated on news and events, do subscribe to our social media channels:

YouTube - @coachbsr
Facebook - @coachbsr
Instagram - @coach.bsr
Twitter - @coachbsr
LinkedIn - @coachbsr
Website: www.coachbsr.com